JOKES:
THEIR PURPOSE
AND MEANING

JOKES:
THEIR PURPOSE
AND MEANING

Herbert S. Strean

JASON ARONSON INC.
Northvale, New Jersey
London

Production Editor: Judith D. Cohen

This book was set in 11 point Palacio by Lind Graphics of Upper Saddle River, New Jersey, and printed and bound by Haddon Craftsmen of Scranton, Pennsylvania.

Library of Congress Cataloging-in-Publication Data

Strean, Herbert S.
    Jokes : their purpose and meaning / by Herbert S. Strean.
      p. cm.
    Includes bibliographical references (p.) and index.
    ISBN 1-56821-070-1
    1. Wit and humor—Psychological aspects. I. Title.
RC489.H85S77 1994
152.4—dc20   93-17050

Manufactured in the United States of America. Jason Aronson Inc. offers books and cassettes. For information and catalog write to Jason Aronson Inc., 230 Livingston Street, Northvale, New Jersey 07647.

To Marcia,
the better half of this book,
with love

Contents

Preface:
Laughing Matters

Ever since I could form and understand words, I have been very busy telling and listening to jokes. Relatives, friends, and colleagues often greet me with their latest joke. Some groan when I greet them with my latest joke. I don't think I have ever taught a class without telling at least one joke and I doubt if I have ever attended a professional meeting without an exchange of jokes with colleagues.

When I reminisce about important individuals in my life, I'll often remind myself of the particular jokes they have told me. Furthermore, of the hundreds of jokes I still recall and frequently relate, I almost always remember who originally told me the joke, and the place and date of the telling. Jokes are so much a part of my daily interactions that when I retired from Rutgers University in 1986, all of the faculty members who "roasted" me had some humorous remark to make about my preoccupation with jokes. I particularly remember the sentiments of my colleague and friend, Dean Ralph Garber, who said, "Herb Strean's compulsion to tell jokes is well known.

The only trouble with it is that every time he tells a joke he laughs in the middle of it and then thinks that is sufficient reinforcement to tell the joke all over again!" Yes, as the old adage goes, "Many a truth is said in jest."

Long before I became aware of the findings of dynamic psychology, I intuitively recognized that many ideas and emotions that we human beings cannot feel free to express directly can be communicated through the medium of jokes. I learned in my early teens that jokes can be used to discharge sexual, aggressive, and other forbidden thoughts and fantasies without worrying about being punished. When I was in college, my initial interest in psychoanalysis began with my reading Sigmund Freud's (1905) *Jokes and Their Relation to the Unconscious*. Freud quickly became a benign superego for me because he gave me permission to enjoy "the forbidden." In college I memorized his statement: "The joke will evade restrictions and [will] open sources of pleasure that have become inaccessible" (p. 103). That sounded most intriguing to a college junior and still does to a senior citizen! I also welcomed Freud's statement: "Even men of eminence . . . are not ashamed in their autobiographies to report their having heard some excellent joke" (p. 15).

When I started my own personal analysis, I told my analyst many jokes. He almost never laughed, and after I expressed my deep hurt, intense indignation, and acute embarrassment, I did not have too many alternatives available to me other than to examine the latent meaning of the jokes I told and to discover the unconscious motives that propelled my telling particular jokes at particular times.

I learned that my reasons for telling jokes were many – strong bids for love and appreciation, a means of coping with anxiety, a disguised way of expressing erotic and hostile wishes, satisfying exhibitionism, and much more. I began to recall that the way I could best induce a positive response from my strict parents was to make them laugh at my jokes; that was what I was trying to repeat in the transference relationship with my analyst. But it didn't work. Yet, I still recall the one joke I told my analyst that did make him laugh:

> A beggar approached a dignified and elegant gentleman and asked, "Mister, would you please give me a quarter for a cup of coffee?" The gentleman responded haughtily, "I gave you a quarter just an hour ago," to which the beggar responded, "Mister, stop living in the past!"

As I subjected that joke to psychoanalytic investigation, I learned that at the time I told it to my analyst, I was feeling like a beggar trying to extract something tangible from him, whom I was experiencing as a withholding parent.

Examining other jokes that came to mind in my analytic sessions revealed different parts of my psychic structure to me—superego commands, habitual defenses, ideals, fantasies, and conflicts. Jokes that interested me, I realized upon examining them, were sources of rich insight, much as dreams and slips of the tongue provide a royal road to the unconscious.

As I studied the meaning and purpose of my own joke-telling, I began to study further dimensions of telling and listening to jokes. I learned that many subtle interpersonal dynamics are at work as one person tells another a joke. I discovered why some individuals frequently laugh at jokes and others rarely do. I learned that transference and countertransference factors are always at work as jokes are being related. For many individuals, including myself, the act of telling and listening to jokes has many similarities to making love, and the laughter that can erupt can be likened to an orgasm. Further, mutual laughter between two confreres as they exchange jokes can be similar to a mutual orgasm.

Although my lengthy and intensive study of jokes and their vicissitudes has been a labor of love, I have acquired a great deal of conceptual understanding on the subject, which I would like to share with colleagues and friends. Specifically, I would like to discuss with the readers of this book some of the major properties of a "good" joke—double meaning, incongruity, surprise, deriding an enemy, and more, which I have observed on my journeys to "jokeland."

A phenomenon that has particularly interested me is why some individuals remember most jokes told to them and why others forget them right away. I have also been interested in understanding better why some individuals can enjoy the same joke many times and others cannot tolerate hearing a joke more than once. These and other human responses to jokes will be discussed in this book.

Although I have discovered that many individuals like to tell jokes and most like to listen to them, there are some who hate to do either. I remember first becoming aware of the hatred that some men and women have toward jokes in the 1960s when I was a young professor at Rutgers University. At the beginning of the semester in a doctoral seminar on personality theory, one of the students asked me in class, "What do we have to do to get an 'A'?" I answered, "Participate in class, write a good term paper, and laugh at my jokes!" I didn't think much about that until, late in the semester, one of the doctoral candidates came into my office in tears and inquired, "Are you going to flunk me?" With enormous surprise I asked, "Why would you think I would do that?" "Because," said the student, " I didn't think your jokes were funny and I didn't laugh at them!"

Yes, some people lack a sense of humor! They cannot laugh at themselves or with others. These are the individuals who frown on hearing a joke, or if they want to be polite, will say, "I don't get it." Who are these people? What can we say about their psychodynamics? These and other questions we hope will be answered in this text.

In my professional work, I have found that the problem-ridden issues that are frequently brought to the psychotherapist's office, such as in sex, marriage, parent–child interactions, race and religion, and psychotherapy are expressed in one way or another in most of the jokes that individuals tell each other. Consequently, the jokes in this book that I will examine with readers will be concerned with the hopes, conflicts, fantasies, pain, and anxiety that most patients bring to psychotherapists.

In Chapter 1, I will discuss some of the components of "good" jokes, show their common properties, and particularly try to demonstrate how unconscious fantasies, wishes, defenses, and superego injunctions are expressed in jokes. I will deal with issues such as how knowing an individual's favorite joke can be of much diagnostic value to the therapist and how and why successful psychotherapy frequently strengthens a patient's ability to laugh and make others laugh. As in all of the chapters of this book, there will be many jokes told, illustrating particular dynamic principles.

Chapters 2 through 6 will consist, respectively, of jokes on sex, marriage, parent–child relations, race and religious issues, and psychotherapy. In each chapter I will try to convey to the reader some of the unconscious meanings of a particular joke and some of the motives one has in telling it and enjoying hearing it told. Of course, we realize a particular joke has unique meaning to each listener and to each teller. Yet, we know there are reasons why certain jokes remain popular through several generations. Obviously these jokes have a meaning and purpose for all of us and many of these classic jokes will be on the pages of this book.

I would like to express my thanks to several people who have been very helpful to me in producing this book. First and foremost, I would like to express my loving appreciation to my wife Marcia, who has traded jokes with me for over forty years, and who has also typed and edited this book. My sons Dr. Richard Strean and Dr. Billy Strean, in addition to sharing many good jokes with me, have taught me how to tell jokes with more skill, and have shown me on many occasions why my presentation of a joke did not elicit the results I was striving for. I owe a debt of gratitude to the many friends, relatives, and colleagues who have shared jokes with me on many occasions and for many years. Finally, I would like to thank Jason Aronson and his staff for helping me put my labor of love into print.

1

Jokers Are Wild: An Introduction to Jokers and Their Jokes

Since the beginning of recorded time, telling and listening to jokes have been popular practices. It is well known that almost all societies, cultures, ethnic groups, families, and individuals have their favorite jokes and enjoy relating them.

It is not surprising that exchanging jokes is as old as human civilization because doing so serves many constructive purposes for most men, women, and children. Telling and listening to jokes give us an opportunity to play, to regress, to depart from the demands of reality, and to enjoy the child in ourselves and in others. The laughter that often emerges when a joke is related frequently reduces intrapsychic and interpersonal tensions. Furthermore, relating and hearing a joke often brings individuals closer to each other, inasmuch as the themes, conflicts, and characters in most jokes foster mutual identification and empathy between the parties. Telling and listening to jokes, therefore, can enhance object relations and self-esteem, and diminish frustration, anxiety, and hatred among people.

Strangers often become friendlier after an exchange of jokes.

Lecturers, teachers, and chairpersons are usually sensitive to the fact that a joke can break the ice and induce warm receptivity in the audience. Spouses, parents, children, and estranged friends and relatives have long recognized that telling jokes can help to puncture old antagonisms and provide an atmosphere that is conducive to constructive problem-solving. Exchanging jokes, in effect, is good for our mental health. As Martin Grotjahn (1957) pointed out in *Beyond Laughter*, by speaking to and from the unconscious, exchanging jokes gives people more freedom in a culture that fosters repression.

Although joke-telling is a human activity as old as mankind, it is a subject that has been very much neglected in the psychotherapeutic literature. A computer search on clinical subjects such as "rage," "sexuality," and "hostility" yields over five hundred entries. "Humor," "laughter," and "wit" combined yield a mere thirty-three (Satow 1991).

Despite the fact that the father of psychotherapy, Sigmund Freud, gave a great deal of thought to the purposes and meaning of jokes, and told many of them to students, colleagues, relatives, and even to his patients, his book *Jokes and Their Relation to the Unconscious*, written in 1905, is still the most definitive work on the subject by a psychotherapist. Other attempts by clinicians (for example, Bergler 1956, Grotjahn 1957, Kris 1952, Reik 1954, 1962, Wolfenstein 1954) tend to rehash Freud's notions and, in many instances, repeat the jokes he related in *Jokes and Their Relation to the Unconscious*.

When we note that jokes reflect some of the most problematic, painful, exciting, and personal aspects of human existence, it is quite surprising that mental health professionals have given such limited attention to them. Indeed, the "best" jokes, the ones that bring out a lot of laughter, invariably deal with issues that the psychotherapist confronts daily—sexual desires, aggressive fantasies, marital conflicts, disturbed parent–child interaction, interpersonal strife among members of different races and religions, and anxiety coping with psychotherapy and psychotherapists. Furthermore, the jokes that an individual enjoys telling and/or hearing can give us a great deal of insight into that person (Zwerling 1955). Spalding (1978), a humorist who is not a mental health professional, in his book *American Jewish Humor* suggests that if somebody tells you what he or she laughs at, you can tell who that person is.

Many writers have pointed out that it is not difficult to reveal dominant characteristics of individuals or cultures if we sensitize ourselves to what makes them laugh. The humorist Sam Levenson (1979) in *You Don't Have to Be in Who's Who to Know What's What* has suggested that the jokes we like to tell and hear reflect our defiances, challenges, and denunciations. Leo Rosten (1961) defined the telling of jokes as "the affectionate communication of insight" (p. 15).

There are probably many reasons to explain why mental health professionals have devoted such limited attention to jokes and wit in general. Those who are interested in the subject tend to be preoccupied with the defensive aspects of laughter and humor. Greenson (1967), for example, has pointed out that attempts to engage in humorous exchanges during treatment may signify the patient's resistance to acknowledging hateful feelings toward the therapist. Satow (1991) has suggested that the popularity of the classical Freudian model among clinicians has made them "cynical about humor in group or individual treatment" (p. 242). She suggests that with the advent of object relations theory and self psychology, more practitioners will be able to appreciate the mastery-building aspects of laughing as well as the data it can provide on the individual's object relations.

The use of humor in and out of the therapeutic setting as conceptualized by many professionals seems to have many pejorative implications. It has been viewed as acting out (Reich 1949), a form of seduction (Fenichel 1945), and almost always as a resistance to treatment (A. Freud 1946). It was only quite recently that a classical psychoanalyst viewed the expression of humor in the treatment situation as a step forward by the patient in his or her analysis. In his highly creative and scholarly paper, "The Gift of Laughter: On the Development of a Sense of Humor in Clinical Psychoanalysis," Warren Poland (1990) points out:

> the capacity for humor linked to wisdom about the world is available in varying degrees to all of us, and one of the special delights of clinical analysis is seeing the liberation and development of such humor in the course of a patient's analytic work. [p. 197]

Poland takes the position that as a patient matures, there is an increased ease in being amused. He implies that as patients are more capable of accepting themselves, they become more capable of laughing at themselves and at the world. He concludes: "It is not a perfect world or an ideal world, but we deal with it as best we can and even find delight in that. Such a mature level of delight is the quality [termed] the gift of laughter" (p. 199).

Inasmuch as joking involves playing and therefore requires a suspension of secondary processes, psychotherapists who champion sound reality testing, mature judgment, and good impulse control may consider a preoccupation with jokes as being too childish. For many decades mental health professionals tended to adopt the paradigm of the wise, mature doctor ministering to the sick, immature patient as an appropriate model for conducting psychotherapy. Now that clinicians are moving toward conceptualizing the psychotherapeutic relationship as consisting of two vulnerable human beings interacting and each capable of appearing infantile (Strean 1991, 1993), they may become more willing to relate to the joker that is in every patient and every therapist. As practitioners begin to consider the medical model of the healthy doctor and the sick patient as obsolete, they may become more accepting of Harry Stack Sullivan's (1953) maxim, "We are all more human than otherwise," and therefore see the capacity to appreciate humor as involving adaptive ego strengths and a superego that can be benign.

What Is a Joke?

According to the college edition of *The Winston Dictionary* (1943), a joke is "something said or done to cause mirth; a witticism; jest" (p. 531). As I have already suggested, the joke in every culture is the surest and best way to induce laughter. In his *Giant Book of Laughter*, Rosten (1985) defines the joke as "a very short short story, carefully structured, a very brief narrative designed to reach a comedic climax through skillful cues, deliberate miscues, and sudden surprise" (p. 1). A good joke, according to Rosten, uses camouflage with creative cunning. What this entails is "the disguising of purpose, the distribution of tantalizing but misleading 'leads,' the planting of totally deceptive expectations. All of these elements must combine to explode in the surprise of that laughter Hobbes called 'sudden glory'" (p. 2). Freud (1905) alleged that jokes combined playful disappointment with satisfaction. The joke reflects the human being's ability to make the best of a bad thing, an act of aggressive resignation.

Jokes can be defined in many ways because they combine many properties and satisfy a variety of motives. It is the aim of this chapter to consider some of the major characteristics of jokes and to reflect also on their intrapsychic and interpersonal meaning to those who relate them and listen to them.

One of the most obvious pleasures involved in exchanging jokes is that it involves play. The norms that govern reality are abandoned for a while and the joking partners break the rules.

Those who enjoy jokes like to play with words. Words offer many opportunities to play and one way of playing with words is to tell jokes with double meanings.

Jokes with Double Meanings

When children begin learning right from wrong, they are concomitantly learning the meaning of words. During their second year of life, as they are toilet trained and helped to master some of the other requirements of reality, serious verbal communication begins. Just as the toddler takes pride in his or her ability to establish sphincter control, he or she takes a similar pride in producing the right words for the right concept. Those of us who have lived with and/or treated children have often recognized that 2-year-olds show off their verbal abilities in the same way they exhibit their toilet training successes. When my 2-year-old son Richard was in his stroller returning from a walk in New York City's Central Park, he and his mother met the internationally renowned psychoanalyst Dr. Theodor Reik in the lobby of our building. My wife said to Richard, "I'd like you to meet a very famous man, Theodor Reik." Dr. Reik, with his characteristic charm said, "Hello, Richard. It's nice to meet you." That evening when my wife and I were leaving to go to see a play, and I said, "Bye, Richard, Mommy and I are going to the theater," Richard replied, "Theater Reik?"

Despite the fact that youngsters enjoy mastering the requirements of reality, they resent its restrictions and impositions. That is why the modal 2-year-old is very negativistic and goes through the "No" stage often called *the terrible twos*. As 2-year-olds defy parents and other adults, they delight in finding fault with how words are used and they often misuse them purposely. I remember when my younger son Billy was 2, in place of the word "Yes" he would, with a twinkle in his eye, say "S-E-Y," spelling it backwards not to be too cooperative.

I believe that the psychological roots of telling jokes lie in our wish to be a 2-year-old again and play with words, show off our skills, and simultaneously defy the world in a way that will not bring on too much retribution. It might even bring approbation. Many, perhaps most, jokes that we tell give us the opportunity to play, show off, and defy. We can be, to some extent, 2 years old again.

Children love to tell jokes in which the words are used in two ways, or as Freud (1905) pointed out, "play upon words which have a double meaning" (p. 37). There are a number of these jokes available.

> A mother asks her young daughter, "Did you take a bath this morning?" The child responds, "Why, is one missing?"

In this girl's terse response, she is playing, exhibiting, and defying, and only needs four words to do it all. The young daughter at a tender age has learned that "brevity is the soul of wit." She agrees with Freud who said that the best joke is the short joke.

> The man who is greeted by a friend he hasn't seen for a while, "Say, your hair is getting thin," responds, "Well, who wants fat hair!"

Reiterating, in order to enjoy telling and listening to jokes, we must keep the child alive in us and enjoy that child. We must also be able to enjoy the child in our confreres so that we can laugh together. If we can permit ourselves to regress, we will continue to look for and pleasurably relate many humorous stories that have double meaning. Here are some that adults have enjoyed.

> A minister who had to endorse a check, but was unfamiliar with fiscal matters, wrote on the back, "I heartily endorse this check."

The double meaning of the word *endorse* in the joke is used to demean the minister and expose his naïveté. As virtually anyone who has studied the dynamics of joke-telling has discovered, and a point on which we will elaborate throughout this book, almost all jokes give the teller and the audience an opportunity to deride and demean someone. As we will discuss in Chapter 2 when we study sexual jokes, hostility and contempt often appear in sexual interactions. Double meaning is used in the following two sexual jokes.

> A young man pursues a young lady to get her to bed. She angrily confronts him, "I won't stand for it!" He expresses relief because the church he belongs to doesn't permit sex standing up because it could lead to dancing.

The next joke describes an event that is really supposed to have occurred, but I will not vouch for it.

> The great actor Boris Tomashevsky was ending his evening with a prostitute. He reaches into his pocket and says, "Here are two tickets to my next performance!" The woman says, "Thank you, but Boris, I need money, I need bread." "The great actor Boris Tomashevsky gives tickets to his performance. You want bread? Fuck a baker!"

Here is a joke/riddle that depends on double meaning, which gave people an opportunity to discharge hostility during the 1992 presidential campaign:

> Question: What is the difference between John Gotti and George Bush? Answer: John Gotti has at least one conviction!

Some More Riddles

One of the features frequently characteristic of a joke is its riddlelike quality. Children especially love to tell riddles. It gives them a wonderful opportunity to be in the driver's seat, a role usually proscribed by their elders. When children can be the questioner rather than the one required to answer, they "identify with the aggressor" (A. Freud 1946) and feel superior to whomever they ask the riddle. It gives them the opportunity to be the boss, ask the question, and be the smart one who knows the answer, all at the same time!

Some riddles capitalize on the use of double meanings. Here are two:

> Question: Why did the turtle cross the street? Answer: To get to the Shell station.

> Question: What has more lives than a cat? Answer: A frog that croaks every night.

Or, another possible answer I have heard to the second riddle, "Two cats."

Because riddles help the teller feel smarter, something we all want to feel, children have created many "moron" jokes. By making fun of somebody stupid, the child, by contrast, feels intelligent. Moron stories often capitalize on the double-meaning technique.

> Question: How did the moron get a bump behind his head? Answer: He was putting toilet water behind his ears when the seat fell down.

> Question: What did one moron say to the other moron? Answer: I've got more on than you.

> Question: Why did the moron climb on his neighbor's roof? Answer: He heard the drinks were on the house.

Sometimes the riddlelike quality of a joke does not require an answer, as in:

> Does the name Pavlov ring a bell?

Or

"Great Scott! I've forgotten who wrote *Ivanhoe!*" and "Who the Dickens wrote *A Tale of Two Cities?*"

Also, humor can be found when a question is the answer. Here's an example.

Question:: How's your wife? Answer: Compared to whom?

Deriding the Use of Certain Language

Many jokes deride an individual's use of highfalutin language. Our pleasure in demeaning someone trying to sound superior probably comes from our childhood when we felt small and vulnerable, thus hostile or envious toward bigger people who used big words that made us feel inferior. On occasion, the child in us wants to humiliate an individual who comes across as a know-it-all. When my sons were college students, coping with professors and others whom they may have considered superior to them, they enjoyed the following joke (a story that probably actually occurred on a campus somewhere).

A newly arrived freshman at Princeton, an African-American, asks an upperclassman in the quad, "Say, fella, can you tell me where the library's at?" The Princetonian responds, "At Princeton, we don't end sentences with a preposition!" "Oh," the freshman replies, "then can you tell me where the library's at, asshole?"

As I listened to this joke with much pleasure, and saw that others did too, it occurred to me that the joke offers a wonderful opportunity to the many of us who want to hate an oppressor with impunity.

As we know, and will discuss further in Chapter 6, we psychotherapists are often the butt of jokes because we pose a threat to the security of many people. Often the therapist's use of language is the focus of jokes.

> A rather naïve lady was in psychotherapy because she had many sexual problems. Her therapist, trying to liberate her with many id interpretations, kept calling attention to her "phallic" competition, her deep yearning to have a "phallus," her envy of a "phallus." After several sessions of this, the lady turned to the therapist and asked, "Tell me, what is a 'phallus'?" Being a modern therapist, he pulled down his pants to show her. "Oh," the patient said pointing to it, "It's the same as a penis, only smaller!"

Although we can deride sophisticated speakers by criticizing what we feel are their pretentiousness and arrogance, their erudition can arouse laughter. It is funny when we contrast the sophisticated speaker to his confrere's simplicity.

> A New Yorker, very fond of fish, asked his taxicab driver in the Midwest, "Can I get scrod here?" "Sure," responded the cab driver, "but I never heard it in the pluperfect subjunctive before."

Many of the jokes that demean verbose speakers have a sexual context. We contrast their intellectualized demeanor with our earthy approach to what comes naturally.

> A coed comes home from her freshman year and tells her parents she's pregnant. When the mother of the girl asks who is the father, and the girl doesn't know, the mother says, "Why didn't you ask your role partner, 'With whom am I having the pleasure?'"

Highfalutin words are sometimes used by earthy sexual people so that the contrast between their usual demeanor and their elegant words arouses our laughter. Executives make a particularly good audience for this one.

A gentleman visits a house of prostitution and is greeted by the madam. She accompanies him up two flights of stairs to a room, and begins to get undressed. The man protests, "But you are not supposed to do this. You're the madam here." The madam answers, "Intermittently I like to get away from administration."

Slips of the Tongue

As we examine the many psychological facets of exchanging jokes and appreciate how playing with words very often constitutes a major part of the exchange, we begin to realize that jokes bear many similarities to slips of the tongue. Moore and Fine (1990) in *Psychoanalytic Terms and Concepts* define slips of the tongue as "compromise formations between forbidden impulses or ideas and the censorship imposed on them. . . . [They are] tendencies particularly subject to conflict involving sexuality, aggression, strength or weakness, control or lack of control" (p. 139).

In slips of the tongue, we substitute a word we did not consciously intend for one we intended to use. The slip in effect conveys a double meaning to what we say. Playing with words while joking allows us to regress and relinquish certain restraints; so too, slips of the tongue have a similar psychological purpose. We laugh at the slips we hear because the slip usually reveals a forbidden truth that emerges from repression—sometimes causing the speaker embarrassment but frequently giving the audience an opportunity to laugh as they see somebody "caught with his or her pants down."

In Idaho during the 1988 presidential campaign, George Bush enthusiastically described his relationship with President Reagan. "For seven and a half years I have worked alongside him, and I am proud to be his partner. We have had triumphs, we have made mistakes, we have had sex."

> After a stunned moment, Mr. Bush hastily corrected himself and said, "We have had setbacks."

When George Bush slipped and said "sex" instead of "setbacks," we might conjecture that the forbidden truth that emerged from his unconscious was the fact that he felt "screwed" for many years. As Bush was about to say good-bye to his boss, he may have felt a little safer to tell the truth about how he felt being a vice president to Reagan for eight years. Through his slip, he came a little closer to doing so.

Although slips of the tongue and jokes reveal hidden truths, they are usually truths that the maker of the slip feels are too dangerous to assert. My colleague, Dr. Robert Barker (1987), in *The Social Work Dictionary* gives an excellent example of a slip that occurred in the therapeutic situation:

> A client, who feared that a social work investigator was going to reduce some welfare benefits, referred to the investigator as the "social worrier." [p. 116]

Just as we have seen that playing with words can offer an outlet for hostility, slips of the tongue can be unconsciously arranged for the same purpose.

On several occasions when speaking to groups who had some reservations about my point of view, I found that the resentment toward me took the form of slips of the tongue. The superficial politeness that was almost always present was betrayed by the hostility that emerged in the slips. They evoked laughter in practically everyone except the maker of the slip. Just prior to going on a television program called "Straight Talk," the interviewer had made it clear that she had strongly disagreed with all I had written in my book *Resolving Marital Conflicts*. When we finally went on camera, she was prepared to introduce me as "a distinguished professor from Rutgers University." Instead she announced, "Dr. Strean is a disgusting professor from Rutgers University."

Once a colleague who disagreed with many of my ideas wanted to say, "I now present Dr. Strean." Instead, he said, "I now prevent Dr. Strean."

When I was on tour to promote a book, the same woman introduced me to three different audiences. She must have started to resent this because during the second introduction, when she meant to say, "Dr. Strean makes difficult ideas sound easy," she said, "Dr. Strean makes easy ideas sound difficult." On the third introduction her latent resentment emerged quite clearly as she told the audience, "To miss hearing Dr. Strean speak is the chance of a lifetime."

In my psychotherapeutic work and in teaching, I have found that humorous slips of patients, students, and of mine usually revealed hidden resistances, transferences, and countertransferences. A prospective patient called me on the phone and said, "I'm desperately in need of trouble," instead of what he consciously wanted to say, that he desperately needed help. This man turned out to be severely paranoid and had delusions of persecution, obsessing daily that his wife was having an extramarital affair. His slip reflected his anxiety in being a potent man with his wife. Consequently, he unconsciously arranged to feel rejected by her. Fantasying his wife in bed with another man was a form of "trouble" that protected him from experiencing incestuous fantasies and was his maladaptive manner of coping with oedipal conflicts.

A graduate student of mine whom I always thought was anti-Semitic wrote in an evaluation of the class I taught, "The professor was adept in teaching us psychosexual development. I particularly enjoyed the material he presented on the oral, anal, and gentile periods."

I was a young practitioner in the early 1950s when I was assigned an extremely attractive dancing instructor from Arthur Murray's Dancing School who aroused sexual fantasies in me. I tried hard to suppress my erotic countertransference reactions, but in presenting the case to a seminar I said, "After a few months of therapy, she came to the sessions with her overcoat on, as if trying to control my impulses." I wanted to say "her impulses."

Over the years, as I have tried to determine how a particular joke became one, I have thought that some jokes might have had their origin as slips of the tongue. While pondering this issue, I found myself making many slips and then as an aid in recovering from my embarrassment, I would often turn the slips into a further play on words. The following might be considered a "triple play" on words. The mother of our son Richard's friend called our home one day. I answered the phone, and after going through the usual social amenities, she proudly informed me that her new boyfriend was a well-known baseball player. As I pictured her boyfriend, a provocative tobacco-chewing ball player, with her, an erudite professor, I felt skeptical about the future of their relationship. My doubts emerged in a slip of the tongue when I said without thinking, "I find it hard to believe that you can get to first base with him." I felt my face redden when she responded, "Where did that come from?" To aid in my recovery from revealing what I did not want to, I responded, "From left field." Now speaking seriously, she said, "You help people with marriage. What do you suggest?" I answered, "Sacrifice!" When the woman said, "You know, we still have separate houses," I proclaimed, "You better watch out he doesn't steal home!"

The following jokes, I have hypothesized, may have started out as slips of the tongue.

> A young man confesses to a priest that he tried to kiss a nun. The priest is very forgiving, but reminds the parishioner, "I'll forgive you but don't get into the habit."

> Question: What does Madonna lack, the Pope has but doesn't use, and Arnold Schwarzenegger uses all the time? Answer: A last name.

> An Indian boy asks his father, Black Cloud, "Where do we get our names?" His father explains, "When a baby is born,

the first thing seen outside the wigwam becomes the baby's name. Such as Budding Tree, or Dark Earth. But, you should know that, Two Dogs Fucking . . ."

Returning to baseball, I have wondered if the following joke originated in a slip of the tongue.

Two Englishmen were at a cricket match when one told the other, "You should observe the Americans play baseball." "How do they play?" asked his friend. "Well, a chap with a mallet hits a pellet into the far meadow. That's known as a home run. One day I observed a chap take a stroll to the first mound. He was walked." "Why?" asks the gentleman hearing about American baseball. His knowledgeable friend answers, "Because he had four balls." "Gracious," says the student. "With that impediment he should have been carried!"

My wife tells me that when she was in college she had to fill out a questionnaire in her dormitory. Where the form asked for "church preference," she wrote in "Brick."

I recall the time when I was a consultant to the staff at a county Department of Public Welfare. On a face sheet a client filled out name, address, etc. Following "Sex," she wrote "3 × a week."

And, of course, there's Yogi Berra's famous slip when he began his speech for "Yogi Berra Day" in his hometown of St. Louis: "I just want to thank everyone who made this day necessary."

What radio and television commentators call "bloopers" are really slips of the tongue. Three of my favorites: "It's a privilege to present to you now the distinguished Virgin of Governor's Island." "I am very happy to speak to you over this nationwide hiccup." A radio master of ceremony introducing the actor, Walter Pidgeon: "Mr. Privilege, this is indeed a pigeon."

I remember reading a composition by a teenager who ended

his romantic story with "They were married and lived happily even after."

In a newspaper write-up of a wedding reception, the reporter wrote, "The bride and her mother were in the deceiving line."

I don't remember in which college newspaper I read this typo: "The report was signed by five faulty members of the university."

I am told the following event actually occurred in a therapy session:

> A patient confessed, "Doctor, last night I made a Freudian slip." Delighted with his patient's involvement in the treatment process, the therapist asked, "What was the slip?" "Well," the patient explained, "I was having dinner with my mother and wanted to say, 'Mother, please pass the butter.' Instead, I said, 'Mother you are a bitch. I hate your guts.'"

This last vignette, like most jokes, contains an element of incongruity, which is a frequent, if not essential, property of jokes. Let us examine its contribution to laughter in more detail.

Incongruity

Similar to dreams in this regard, jokes contain both rational and irrational elements. In dreams and jokes, something divorced from reality is coupled with a rational thought or dialogue. Standing side by side in a peculiar, noncomplementary manner, in jokes we observe fantasy coinciding with reality, secondary processes merging with primary processes, and mature behavior being coupled with regressive modes of adaptation. An incongruous situation such as one in which an elegant gentleman adorned in an expensive tuxedo, but simultaneously wearing a dirty football helmet, amuses us. We chuckle at the seeming incongruity of a nun cursing, or a boxer reciting poetry. Sid Caesar and Milton Berle, world-renowned comedians, were masters of incongruity and brought it into their great acts.

In *Laughing: A Psychology of Humor*, Norman Holland (1982) suggests that in jokes there is always something affirmed and something denied. Often it is the same proposition such as in the following story:

> An elderly gentleman enters a doctor's office. When asked what is his problem, the man answers, "I can't pee." The doctor asks, "How old are you?" When the man answers, "I'm 92," the doctor retorts, "You've peed enough!"

In the above example, urinating is both affirmed and denied. As Holland (1982) has pointed out, in a joke something is not only affirmed and denied, but it is also valued and devalued simultaneously. The merging of two things that do not fit, that is, are incongruent, is what makes us laugh. Freud (1905), in alluding to incongruity in jokes, suggested that "playful disappointment" is combined with satisfaction.

In the musical *Fiddler on the Roof*, a beggar approaches a businessman and asks for a handout. The businessman declares, "I can't give you anything. I've had a bad week." The beggar admonishes the man, "Just because you've had a bad week, why should *I* suffer?"

The coupling of contrasts is clearly seen in the above joke. Though the beggar is obviously a man of low socioeconomic status, he has the arrogance to feel entitled to a handout. We also see the regressed and demanding attitude of a baby coupled with the fact that the beggar is obviously a mature adult. As Freud (1905) also pointed out, a joke "has an appearance of logic about it, which, as we already know, is a suitable facade for a piece of faulty reasoning" (p. 60).

Another way of looking at the incongruity in a joke is to

realize that a piece of absurdity is merged with reality. If
something is absurd in isolation, it is much less amusing than
when it is brought together with something sensible. And, as
we know, sensibility by itself rarely if ever evokes laughter. It
is the combination of both sense and nonsense that brings us
pleasure. It is as if we are still adults but can concomitantly
enjoy being a child, still be rational souls, but are able nonetheless to give ourselves a respite and be frivolous, still be sane
but able to appreciate the insanity in ourselves and others.
These "double features," I believe, are quite apparent in the
following story:

> Mr. Smith gets out of his car to deliver a package to his
> partner's home, a lovely ranch house. It's raining cats and
> dogs and by the time he gets to the door where he is
> greeted by his partner's wife, he is drenched. She tells him
> her husband has left, but he should come in and she will
> give him a cup of hot tea while she dries his clothes in the
> dryer. One thing leads to another and they end up in bed.
> Suddenly, she hears her husband opening the door, so she
> opens the window and shoves Smith out. He looks out to
> the street and sees a group of men jogging, and decides to
> join them. One jogger looks at him and says, "Do you
> usually jog in the nude?" "Yes," says Mr. Smith. "Do you
> always wear a condom?" the jogger inquires. Mr. Smith
> responds, "Only when it rains."

I have observed that the more an interpersonal situation
activates pain for us, as it can in sex, marriage, parent–child
relationships, religion, and psychotherapy (the subject matter
of this book), the more jokes we will find depicting the stresses
from the particular interpersonal area of life being considered.
Think of the incongruity in the following anecdotes that reflect
the conflict, inconsistency, and disorganization in the dimension of life being discussed:

> Mrs. Schwartz was sitting on the stoop of her apartment
> building with her friend, Mrs. Rosenkrantz. While the

ladies were involved in intense conversation, a florist interrupted them to find out if one of the two ladies was Mrs. Schwartz. On learning who she was, the messenger gave her a card that says, "To my darling wife, Love, Abe." "Humph," whines Mrs. Schwartz, "now I'll have to spend the weekend with my legs apart!" In a serious tone Mrs. Rosenkrantz inquires, "What's the matter, you don't have a vase?"

Mr. Harrod was placing some flowers by his wife's grave and noticed Mr. Mason putting a pot of hot soup by his wife's grave. Disdainfully, Harrod says, "You fool, you think your wife can taste that soup?" Mason replies, "When *your* wife smells the flowers, *my* wife will taste the soup."

A mother watching her son graduating from a military academy leans over to her husband and says, "Aren't you proud of our son—of all the two hundred graduates, he's the only one marching in step."

The incongruity in these jokes reflects the anguish, despair, and tension involved in sex, marriage, and parent–child relationships. Consider the incongruity in the following jokes, the first relating to religious conflict, the second depicting some of the discomfort a prospective patient experiences when seeking out a therapist:

A Roman Catholic church had difficulty finding a janitor. Despite misgivings, the trustees decided to hire Mr. Cohen. After working for a week, he was summoned to the Mother Superior's office for a conference. The Mother Superior said, "Mr. Cohen, you are doing a good job. However, there are a few things to straighten out. First, Mr. Cohen, that is the cross of Jesus; please do not hang your coat on it! Second, Mr. Cohen, that is holy water; please do not drink it. And finally, please don't call me 'Mother Shapiro'!"

> Walking into a therapist's office for the first time, a middle-aged man with his hand across his chest inside his jacket is asked his name by the therapist. "I am Napoleon." The therapist asks, "How can I help you, Napoleon?" The gentleman responds, "Oh, *I* don't need any help. It's my wife Josephine—she thinks she's Mrs. Schwartz."

As we reflect further on the incongruity that characterizes the jokes discussed in this section, we can infer that incongruity is a global concept that comprises many human qualities. It embraces grandiosity, surprise, denial, mockery, and many other human responses to life's trials and tribulations. All of them are the dominant themes of the stories and anecdotes we call jokes, which evoke our laughter. They are similar to the latent content in dreams, and by examining them further we gain more understanding of jokers and their jokes.

Grandiosity

As most mental health professionals learn, and as the father of modern psychotherapy has carefully documented in "Analysis Terminable and Interminable" (Freud 1937a), all human beings have enormous difficulty coping with their grandiose wishes. All of us want to be kings, queens, princes, or princesses. To give up the pleasure principle and cease being omnipotent babies who get what we want when we want it, is a feat no one fully accomplishes. We resent frustration, we abhor criticism, and we hate to be unloved. If we are told we are wrong about something, even when we recognize that we have been in error, it is most difficult to acknowlege the truth. We human beings want to be perfect and want life to be perfect for us.

For all of the aforementioned reasons, and more, there are many jokes that help us cope with our punctured narcissism and frustrated grandiosity. Among the most popular are those anecdotes that can make us laugh at somebody who is insisting on being in an omnipotent position, which we realize is unrealistic but something we secretly desire.

> Jack Jones tells his friend Bob, "You know, last night I could have had sex with Madonna." "Really," says Bob, "how come?" Jack responds, "Because I had an erection!"

In this joke, Jack is a wonderful example of an adult who wants to be a narcissistic baby. All he has to do is feel excited, and ipso facto he becomes a sexual partner of a national sex symbol. We laugh at Jack because we all would like to be a sexual partner of someone famous we admire but can't get to know. We would rather mock Jack than cope with our own frustrated yearnings.

As we gain experience in doing psychotherapy, we learn many lessons about diagnosing and treating life's conflicts. One of the lessons I was fortunate to learn early in my professional career was that what gives fuel to strong paranoid reactions are strong omnipotent fantasies. I had a young man in therapy who in session after session told me that people were always against him and were out to torment and torture him. It was difficult for me to differentiate the facts from his fantasies and to ferret out reality from what appeared to be his delusions. The uncertainty and anxiety I experienced subsided a little for me when, in a session during the sixth month of treatment, my patient stated with enormous conviction, "When I'm watching the football team go into a huddle, I know for sure they are talking about me."

If an individual wants constant attention but finds human contact unacceptable because the idea creates intense anxiety, he or she is inclined to renounce wishes to love and be loved and, instead, champion hating and being hated. In the above example, my patient secretly wished to he hugged in the football huddle but found the notion unbearable. Consequently, instead of accepting his wish to be part of the huddling team, he made himself an outsider who was hated and rejected.

One does not have to be in psychotherapy to have grandiose fantasies. Longings to be wanted, needed, loved, and important are with us from the womb to the tomb.

> An advertisement appeared in the *New York Times* seeking someone who was "a horseman, a swordsman, and speaks several languages." An older gentleman applied, and the interviewer was skeptical that the man could meet the specific requirements of the job. He asked, "Are you a horseman?" The man answered, "Vot's a horse?" "Well, are you a swordsman?" The man answered, "Vot's a sword?" With annoyance, the interviewer asked, "What languages do you speak?" "Yiddish, and a little Hinglish." The interviewer indignantly asked, "So why did you apply for this job!?" The gentleman answered, "I wanted to let you know, on me you shouldn't depend."

Not only do we want to be loved, adored, wanted, and to be important, but all of us want to be "the one and only." That is why we idealize those who occupy unique and important positions in business and government.

> A man went up to the desk at the Hilton Hotel and asked the clerk for a room. The clerk replied, "I'm sorry, sir, but we don't have any rooms available." "You mean," the man said, "if Bill Clinton came here and asked for a room, you wouldn't have a room for him?" "Well," the clerk said, "for the President of the United States we would find a room." "All right," said the man, "then I'll take his room!"

Another story similar to the one just told:

> Frank Hill bumped into President Kennedy at a hotel and greeted him by saying he had contributed $20,000 to his presidential campaign. Pleased, President Kennedy asked, "Is there something I can do for you?" Mr. Hill answered, "Yes, when I am at dinner tonight with my business

friends, could you just come over to the dinner table in the dining room and say, 'Hi Frank, it's good to see you.'" President Kennedy amicably agreed, and that evening came over to Mr. Hill's table, shook hands with him, and said, "Hi, Frank, it's good to see you." Frank Hill responded, "Look, I'm too busy to talk to you now, call me later."

Surprise

One of the major elements in a story or anecdote that helps make a good joke is surprise. When we are confronted with the unexpected, controls are temporarily suspended, access to primary processes occurs, regression is likely, and we feel like children again. As is well known, children love to surprise and to be surprised.

A joke without surprise is not a joke. It is a story that is without stimulation. It is an event that does not stir up emotions. The more the element of surprise exists in the story, the more we laugh.

> Professor George Brown visited his colleague Professor Peterson in his departmental office at the university. "Where is your secretary?" Brown asked. "I fired her! She was too efficient," answered Peterson. "Too efficient? How can that be?" Professor Brown asked with a puzzled expression on his face. Peterson explained, "You see, last week was my birthday. Did my wife remember it? No. Did my children? No. Did anybody else? No. Only my secretary. She did it right. She took me out for a wonderful dinner at an elegant restaurant with good food, wine, and candlelight. We felt close to each other, and romantic, and then she took me back to her apartment. We were getting very intimate, and she was just about naked, when she excused herself to go into another room. I was taking off my last bit of clothes when she came into the room,

followed by my wife and kids singing, 'Happy Birthday to You'!"

Psychotherapy is full of surprises.

A psychologist was administering some projective tests to Mr. Nelson, trying to determine his sophistication regarding sexual matters. First he asked Mr. Nelson, "What's the difference between men and women?" Mr. Nelson answered, "Men have short hair and women have long hair." To the next question, "What do men do standing up that women do sitting down?" Nelson answered, "Shake hands." Then the psychologist queried, "What do women have two of that cows have four of?" Replied Nelson, "Legs." The psychologist ended the exam saying to Nelson, "Sometimes I get the funniest answers."

Another story drawn from psychotherapy goes as follows:

George White had been in therapy for many years and felt he was making no progress. He finally got up the courage to ask the therapist, "What do you think of me?" "I think you're crazy," answered the doctor. "In that case," said White, "I need a second opinion." The doctor responded, "You're ugly, too!"

Not only are there surprises in resolving situations among men, women, and children, but even among inanimate objects.

Two statues had stood across from each other in Central Park for 100 years. A genie came to the male statue and brought him to life, offering him one wish. He stretched his long-unmoved body with great pleasure, looked around him, and decided on his wish: "Bring her to life, too." The female statue stretched with equal pleasure and they looked at each other. He said, "We have been standing here just looking at each other all this time. Shall we?" "Yes," she said with a gleam in her eye, "Let's!"

"Okay," said the male statue, "you hold the pigeons and I'll shit on them!"

Anyone who plays golf is also in for surprises. Except for outstanding players, after taking a shot it may be difficult to know where your ball lands, and on a public course, to know whom you will meet there.

A duffer sliced his shot into the woods and while looking for his ball came upon an old woman stirring some brew. They greeted each other, and the old woman told the golfer, "If you drink this brew, you can have any wish come true." "Really," said the golfer, "I know what I want. I want to be an outstanding golfer!" The old woman replied, "I can do that for you, but there is one drawback, and that is that you will have very little sex life." "I don't care, I don't care, as long as I can be a great golfer." The golfer drank the brew, and , indeed, he became a nationally famous golfer and won many tournaments. A year later, he hit a ball into the same woods, found the old woman stirring her brew, and told her how appreciative he was because he had become a great golfer. "Yes, but," responded the old woman, "what about your sex life this year?" "Four times," answered the golfer. "See, I told you it would be greatly diminished," said the woman. Replied the golfer, "For a priest in a small town, that's pretty good!"

Denial

When the going gets rough, we do not like to recognize what is happening right before our very eyes. If a sight appears disgusting to us, we tend to overlook it. When something sounds frightening, we may not hear it. If any internal or external event arouses extreme anxiety, we may use the defense mechanism of denial to protect ourselves (A. Freud

1946). The defense is one of the earliest utilized. Infants deny unpleasant stimuli, whether they are uncomfortable bodily stimuli, or external forces that upset their equilibria.

Inasmuch as we adults like to view ourselves as honest, objective, rational souls, we do not enjoy accepting the fact that we can deny the truth. As a matter of fact, when we observe someone else denying the truth, we pejoratively label him or her a liar, and contrast the person with ourselves who are honest and upright. Because denial is a universal phenomenon that we would rather see in others than in ourselves, there are many jokes that along with surprising us and dealing with our grandiose fantasies, also use denial as an important element in making us laugh.

As therapists learn early in their careers, when someone important to a person, such as a son, or daughter, or close friend, goes into therapy, that parent or friend can become quite threatened that he or she will be debased in the treatment or even rejected.

> While conversing over canasta with her friends, Mrs. Stone had to listen to them bragging about their children. One's son just got his Ph.D., another's daughter had married a wealthy businessman, and a third's daughter just was appointed to a political position. Mrs. Stone proudly beamed and said, "You can talk about your children all you want. My Philip is in psychotherapy with an outstanding professional three times a week. And what do they talk about? Only me!"

Similarly,

> When Mrs. Davis asked her son what he learned from his therapist, he replied, "Ma, I got an Oedipus complex." Mrs. Davis shrugged, "Oedipus, shmedipus, as long as you love your mother!"

Because denial is a universal mechanism, we observe it in use practically everywhere we go.

Denying reality, one drunk in a bar seeing another doing pushups on the floor, says to him, "Shay, mishtah, she's gone," as if there had been a woman there.

When a girl came home from college pregnant, her family was extremely upset, her mother hysterical, and her brother yelling at her. Her father tried to calm them and had them sit down to deal with the situation coolly. "Now, first," he said to his daughter, "are you sure it's yours?"

Regardless of the social context in which it takes place, any human event can be denied. Denial can take many different forms.

George, a not very bright man, was standing in a police lineup when they brought in the rape victim. George exclaimed, "That's her all right!"

A British gentleman was strolling in the park when he came across a pile in front of him. "Hmm," he thought, "it looks like shit." He picked some up and smelled it, commenting to himself, "It smells like shit." He tasted it and said, "It tastes like shit. It *is* shit! It's a good thing I didn't step in it."

As we will discuss in more detail in Chapter 4 about parent–child relations, collusion between parents and children in which parents unconsciously aid and abet their youngsters' maladaptive behavior is something virtually all psychotherapists observe daily.

On her first day as a teacher, Miss Smith went around the room introducing herself to each child and giving each a chocolate. When she offered one to Johnny, he refused it saying, "Shove it up your ass!" Miss Smith was humiliated, particularly when the principal, who was observing her, told her he would show her how to deal with such a child. The principal talked to Johnny about his summer and then offered him the candy. Johnny responded, "Shove it up your ass!" Unsuccessful as a role model for the teacher, the infuriated principal called in Johnny's mother for a conference. He explained to Johnny's mother what had happened, and she advised him, "Look, if he doesn't like the candy, fuck 'im!"

Mockery

In discussing several of the properties of a "good" joke, such as denial, surprise, or grandiosity, we may have noted that a major element in virtually all jokes is that someone is being mocked. Johnny's mother demeans the principal. George in the police lineup has the aggression turned against him. Whether it is sadism or masochism, hostility seems to be present in most jokes. In sadistic jokes, the victor triumphantly hurts his or her opponent. In masochistic jokes, there is what Theodor Reik terms "victory through defeat" (1948).

Freud (1905) in *Jokes and Their Relation to the Unconscious* explained quite clearly why disguised hostility is frequently present in the stories and anecdotes that make us laugh.

Since our individual childhood, and similarly, since the childhood of human civilization, hostile impulses against our fellow men have been subject to the same restrictions, the same progressive repression, as our sexual urges. We have not yet got so far as to be able to love our enemies or to offer our left cheek after being struck on the right. . . . Brutal hostility, forbidden by law, has been replaced by verbal invective. . . . [In utilizing] the technique of invective . . . we make our enemy small, inferior, despicable, or comic, we achieve in a roundabout way the enjoyment of overcoming him—to which the third person, who has made no efforts, bears witness by his laughter.

We are now prepared to realize the part played by jokes in hostile aggressiveness. A joke will allow us to exploit something ridiculous in our enemy, which we could not, on account of obstacles in the way, bring forward openly or consciously; once again, then, the joke *will evade restrictions and open sources of pleasure that have become inaccessible.* [pp. 102–103]

Grotjahn (1957) in *Beyond Laughter* stated: "The sophisticated reader will note aggressive trends in every witticism" (p. 10). He further suggested that aggressive wit gives us a new way of admitting dangerous aggression to our consciousness, but is done in a cleverly disguised form. Grotjahn, whose emphasis on aggression in jokes parallels Freud's, clarifies further the work of aggression in jokes.

The first person, the one who makes the joke or perceives the idea, attacks the second person, the butt of the joke. The wish to attack is temporarily repressed, pushed down into the unconscious where it is disguised by the wit work. In order to test whether the work of disguising the aggressive tendency was successful, the first person has to tell his witticism to a third person. The one who has conceived the joke cannot himself laugh, because he is too close to the original aggression and the feeling of guilt about it. The third person, to whom the witticism is told, is only a listener and judges only the disguise of the underlying aggression. This third person becomes guilty only in so far as he is a witness of the aggression but not a participant. He is safely removed from guilt. When the third person, to whom the joke is told, reacts with laughter, the first person, who had originally conceived the witticism, may join him in the laughter with relief: the disguise has succeeded. Hostile jokes lift repressions and open otherwise inaccessible sources of pleasure. [p. 11]

Many writers (Bergler 1956, Greenson 1967, Holland 1982, Reik 1962) have concurred that wit seems to begin with an intention to hurt someone, a wish most cultures require that we repress. Jokes therefore give us a wonderful opportunity to express aggression in a concealed manner toward all kinds of enemies who have made us endure "the slings and arrows of outrageous fortune."

Because aggression is ubiquitous, we find its concealed expression in many jokes describing diverse events in diverse social settings. One of my favorites is alleged to have taken place in the House of Parliament in England in the late 1800s:

> Prime Minister Disraeli and Lord Gladstone were arch enemies who reveled in insulting each other at any opportunity. Gladstone once taunted Disraeli by remarking, "I predict, sir, that you will die on the gallows or from some heinous disease." Disraeli replied, "That depends, my dear sir, whether I embrace your principles or your mistress!"

Even in tiny elevators enormous sadism can be expressed.

> A small man entered an elevator at the same time as a buxom, tall woman. The man sidled up to the woman and said, "What do you say to a little fuck?" She looked down at him and said, "Hello, little fuck."

Somewhat similar is the situation in a tavern:

> A man goes over to a woman he does not know and starts to embrace her and fondle her breasts. She slaps his face, kicks him in the crotch, and pushes him to the floor. Lying there, he looks up at her and says, "I guess a blow job is out of the question?"

Then there's the story of the beggar who plaintively says to a woman passing him on the street, "Lady, I haven't eaten in three days." She continues past him as she says, "Force yourself!"

Masochism is quite obvious in the following story.

> Two immigrants from Russia met in New York City where they were both working in the garment district. They were discussing life in the United States and one said, "America is a very funny country. There's a fellow who comes into the factory, who's 6 feet 8 inches tall. Everyone says to him, 'Hello, Shorty!' Another man is completely bald—he doesn't have a stitch of hair on his head—and they say to him, 'Hello, Curly!' Me, I haven't had a woman in twenty years, they say, 'You fucking Jew.'"

Finally, a piece of mockery of which I was the recipient when I was a faculty member at Rutgers.

> I was recovering from surgery and received the following message in the hospital from my colleagues: "The faculty wishes you a speedy recovery. The vote was 48 to 12."

Sensing Humor

Having reviewed and discussed some of the major properties of jokes, we now consider some of the psychodynamics and interpersonal issues of those who tell jokes and listen to them.

Like many things in life, what decides when a joke becomes a joke is, in the final analysis, in the eyes of the beholder. What is a joke to one person could be a horrendous and upsetting saga to another. As Freud (1905) put it, "Only what I allow to be a joke *is* a joke" (p. 105).

For something to be humorous to the teller and/or the listener, part of the content of the joke has to have a familiar ring. The struggle being described, the impulse concealed, the interpersonal conflict portrayed in the joke must have some significance in the exchange. An obvious example is the ethnic joke. Many Jews will laugh heartily at a joke dealing with anti-Semitism or other struggles of their people. Yet, someone unfamiliar with the hopes, aspirations, values, and religious practices of Jews may not find anything to laugh about (Telushkin 1992).

The pleasure derived from hearing and telling jokes arises "from a purpose being satisfied whose satisfaction would otherwise not have taken place" (Freud 1905, p. 117). Thus, to understand why given individuals appreciate a particular joke, we need to understand something about their forbidden wishes, the flexibility or rigidity of their defenses, the relative degree of benignancy of their superego commands and ego ideals, and something about their current and past family life, to name just a few important variables. Understanding why somebody appreciates a particular joke requires us to conduct the minimum of a good intake interview similar to an initial consultation with a patient.

Elliot Oring (1984) demonstrated in *The Jokes of Sigmund Freud* how a knowledge of Freud's favorite jokes could provide us with some understanding of the character of the founder of psychotherapy, especially because jokes and humor constituted a basic component of Freud's presentation of self. Freud, like all appreciators of jokes, identified with the joke's characters and for him they provided associations to his fantasies and dreams. It has also been reported that important psychoanalytic discoveries were suggested to Freud by jokes. Hans Sachs (1946) in *Freud: Master and Friend* has noted that the concept of sublimation was first suggested to Freud by a humorous cartoon. Oring (1984) points out:

> The fact that Freud was collecting Jewish jokes in 1897 at the very time he was initiating his own self-analysis strongly suggests that these jokes contained personally meaningful messages. [p. 4]

Studying Freud's favorite jokes, Oring (1984) has shown that Freud loved jokes that fell into a few pertinent categories—

those that pertained to beggars (*schnorrers*), marriage brokers (*schadchans*), cleanliness (the *ostjude*), horses (*fahrenheit*), mystical or occult jokes (the *kuck*), and problems around Jewish identity. In linking Freud's favorite jokes to his character, Oring has demonstrated that Freud identified strongly with the beggar inasmuch as his economic position for most of his life was a tenuous one. He was repeatedly forced to accept gifts and loans from friends but, like the beggar, "tended to deny his indebtedness and dependence" (p. 18). Although biographers of Freud such as Jones (1953) and Clark (1980) seemed to paint a picture of harmony in his marriage to Martha, Freud's interest in marriage broker jokes together with other biographical data "point more accurately to a complex of hostile impulses harbored by Freud toward his life-long companion" (Oring 1984, p. 41).

Horses to Freud symbolized his professional career, and both his superstitious beliefs as well as his strong ambivalence about being Jewish (occasionally thinking of himself as a "dirty Jew") are well known (Gay 1979); hence his interest in jokes that contain these themes.

Despite the fact that some writers such as Legman (1968) maintain that one's favorite joke is the definite key to a deep understanding of the joker's personality, I would suggest, as do Oring (1984), Bergler (1956), and Grotjahn (1957), the jokes are one other major source of personality data much like dreams and fantasies.

Although it cannot be averred that by knowing an individual's favorite jokes we have ipso facto found the decisive key to his or her personality functioning, we can say that by becoming familiar with a patient's favorite jokes we can enrich our diagnostic understanding of him or her. When we ask our patients to associate freely to the jokes they tell us, patient and therapist learn a great deal, not only about the patient's dynamics, but about latent transference and countertransference issues, subtle resistances and counterresistances, repressed history, and other data that provide grist for the therapeutic mill.

A single woman in therapy with me for more than a year told me the following joke:

> The prostitutes in Puerto Rico are on strike. They are
> carrying placards that say, "Fuck yourself."

Associating to this joke, much as she would to a dream, my patient was able to get in touch with a lot of repressed sadism toward me. I was the prostitute who was taking her money instead of loving her unconditionally without her having to pay for it. Because I did not gratify her sexually, my patient wanted me to go fuck myself. There were other important issues that we got to by analyzing her association to the joke she told, such as her feeling "used" sexually in and out of therapy, a frustrated romance in Puerto Rico, and other salient material.

An unhappily married man in analysis with me told this joke:

> A husband and wife are having a fierce argument. The
> wife, in a rage, asks, "What would you say if I told you I
> was having an affair with your best friend?" The husband
> replied, "I'd say you were a lesbian."

In associating to this joke, my patient and I first became sensitized to the fact that he wanted to come clean about the extramarital affair he was conducting. In addition, he was hopeful he could clarify his doubts about his wife having an affair. Examining his associations further, the patient was able to recognize some of the bases of his marital conflicts. He started to realize he was in a power struggle with his wife because he was never sure if he or his wife had the penis, that is, the homosexual conflict that provoked the extramarital affair became clarified by his associations to his joke.

Just as the manifest content of a dream cannot reveal everything about the dreamer, but contains many suggestions about him or her, the same is true about an individual's favorite jokes. For those readers who know me personally, they will understand why the joke I am about to tell, one I heard when I was 14 years old, continues to be my favorite. For those who do not know me personally, the manifest content of the joke will provide diagnostic clues about some of my personality dynamics, which I will discuss later.

My Favorite Joke

> Mr. Cohen and Mr. Brown commuted from New Rochelle to New York City every day for twenty years. Although they noticed each other daily, they never exchanged any greeting. Finally, Mr. Cohen approached Mr. Brown and said, "Mister, for tventy years we go back and forth on the same train. Vy we shouldn't make friends?" With a contemptuous air and Harvard accent, Brown replied, "My name is Brown, B-R-O-W-N, Harvard, 1932, from the top of my head to the bottom of my toes, the name is Brown. And my father's name was Brown, B-R-O-W-N, Yale, 1901. From the top of his head to the bottom of his toes, his name was Brown. And my grandfather's name was Brown, B-R-O-W-N, Princeton, 1877. From the top of his head to the bottom of his toes, the name was Brown." Cohen responds, "My name is Cohen, C-O-H-E-N, Dubrovna, 1937. And my fodder's name was Cohen, C-O-H-E-N, Minsk, 1912. And my *zedeh*'s [grandfather's] name was Cohen, C-O-H-E-N, Moscow, 1885. From the top of our heads to the bottom of our toes, ve are all vhite, except in one place, our asshole. There we are brown, b-r-o-w-n."

At the time I heard this joke, I had just moved from Montreal, Canada to New Rochelle. I felt very lonely and, like Mr. Cohen in the joke, I was desperately looking for contact. In seeking friends, I frequently did not receive the response I wanted. My Canadian accent was mocked and my ingratiating demeanor was irritating to many. Yet, I harbored fantasies to hurt those who I felt treated me smugly, much as Cohen repudiated Brown.

So much for the circumstances when I first heard the joke, because they do not explain fully why the joke remains my favorite over a span of close to fifty years. Current circumstances when one hears a joke are like a day's residue that can stimulate a dream, but it does not account for more than a partial explanation.

This joke also links up with my history. In Montreal, I experienced anti-Semitism almost daily. I spent years wanting to mock characters like Brown, but rarely did. Cohen, in the joke, expresses my revengeful fantasies in such a wonderful way.

In this joke, I identify with the underdog, Cohen, whose power struggle is mine. The joke also relates to other more basic dynamics of mine. Throughout my life and to the present I have had strong yearnings to love and be loved, but like Cohen in the joke, I have been cautious about showing my desires. Although I can be and want to be a loyal, loving friend, if I am rebuked I hit back hard, as Cohen did to Brown when his narcissism was punctured. These are a few reasons why the Cohen–Brown story with its focus on a deep desire for human contact, competition, revenge, and problems associated with being Jewish remains my favorite.

Humor: An Ego Strength

Although we have focused up until now on how a joke, similar to a dream or a neurotic symptom, can be dissected to demonstrate personality conflicts at work, it should be remembered that humoring and being humored can be and often are positively adaptive character traits—joking can be viewed often as a regression in the service of the ego (Hartmann 1958). When a joke provides us with pleasure, it induces a condition of triumphant joy. It is a victory of the pleasure principle. The ego, so often required to adapt to reality, resolutely turns away from it and enjoys the uninhibited expression of usually forbidden thoughts and feelings. When we laugh at a joke, the superego relates to the ego as a loving parent does to a child—kind, understanding, and permissive (Grotjahn 1957).

In the Book of Ecclesiastes of the Old Testament is a passage that begins: "For everything there is an appointed time" and ends with "A time to weep, and a time to laugh. . . ." Yet, the Bible is a book full of tears but virtually devoid of laughs. Written probably by individuals who had rigid, punitive superegos, these writers did not possess what Grotjahn (1957) has called the psychological *necessity for irreverence* (p. 25).

In order to have a sense of humor, in order to laugh, libido must be freed from aggression. The one who laughs with others possesses a certain degree of mastery over life's conflicts and enjoys an acceptance of self and others.

A Censor of Humor

In contrast to the individual who has a sense of humor—who possesses some degree of emotional strength, of maturity, of flexibility—is the one who lacks a sense of humor. This individual must submit to the dictates of a rigid, punitive superego. Consequently, the man, woman, or child who censors humor, who cannot laugh, is frequently self-hating, guilt-ridden, and possesses a reservoir of hostility that he or she cannot confront. The eminent psychoanalyst Robert Waelder (1933), in an article "The Psychoanalytic Theory of Play," suggested that the paranoid person, who is always on the alert because he or she fears persecution any minute, cannot relax and play. We can infer from Waelder's notion that those who cannot play cannot exchange jokes. To enjoy jokes requires an acceptance of aggression, not a dread of it; an ability to love, not a repudiation of it. The paranoid person cannot laugh because he or she cannot love! To joke suggests an inner freedom, a certain ability to liberate oneself from some of the pressures of daily living (Roustang 1987).

Jokers and the Joke: An Interpersonal Event

Why does an individual who recalls a particular joke happen to tell it to a particular person at a particular time? Telling jokes and responding to them has many similarities to the interpretive process in psychotherapy when the therapist presents some of his or her own thoughts and the patient reacts to them.

When a patient responds to an interpretation, or to anything else the therapist presents, such as a clarification, confrontation, or question, he or she does not respond just to the content of the material alone. As any experienced clinician knows, patients' responses to their therapists' interventions are very much influenced by their current transference position. If they feel positively and warmly toward the practitioner, there is a strong probability they will accept the therapist's statements as something useful and true regardless of their validity or accuracy. By the same token, if a patient feels negatively toward the therapist, the most brilliant intervention in the world may fall on deaf ears or even exasperate the patient. Finally, if the patient's transference is ambivalent, he or she will partially agree and partially disagree with the practitioner's comments. This is the patient who says, "Yes, but" or "On the other hand."

Just as the content of a joke may contain all of the suitable properties that constitute a good joke, such as surprise, mockery, denial, double meaning, and so forth, if the audience has negative feelings toward the teller of the joke, the joke will probably evoke hisses and other negative responses. Similarly, if the listener to a joke has a positive transference to the teller, even a corny pun can evoke hearty laughter.

In certain important respects, a joke teller who does his or her job well functions like a competent therapist. A sensitive therapist observes, empathizes, and listens carefully to the patient. When the therapist really knows where the patient is, he or she can *time* his or her interventions appropriately. Further, an able therapist knows that unless the patient has some conviction about the issue at hand, the therapist's creative construction will be to no avail. Likewise with an able joke-teller; the latter must be able to know his or her audience well, be sensitive to the listener's moods, feelings, and biases. Telling a joke to someone without an appreciation of who that person is, is like bombarding a patient with a deep id interpretation but without preparing the patient for it. Certain joke tellers induce the same kind of animosity and intense resistance when they tell a "dirty" joke to someone who is not ready for it, as do therapists who tell a patient in the first interview that he or she wants to make mad, passionate love with Mother or Father!

Jokes have their desired effect, that is, laughter, when the teller and the audience are sharing complementary and/or similar feelings and fantasies. For example, I have found that when I sense some latent resentment in a class I am teaching, I can sometimes clear the air by telling a joke in which someone in my position, that is, a person in authority, is mocked. When I am effective, I have the same kind of warm feeling as I do when I make an effective interpretation to a patient who is ready to hear something about his or her resentment toward me.

Over the years, I have become sensitized to the idea that just as each individual has personal likes and dislikes in all areas of life, each individual, if interested in hearing jokes, has his or her joke preferences. My dentist loves to hear anal jokes. A colleague at Rutgers enjoyed only phallic-oedipal jokes. Many people abhor jokes with double meaning; some love them. Joke tellers, like joke listeners, have their favorites and not-so-favorites, too.

There are other similarities between the therapeutic process and joking. Just as many therapists, perhaps most, have a tendency to talk too much in order to diminish their own anxiety, telling jokes can also be used for defensive purposes. I have found myself telling jokes to ward off hostile fantasies, sexual wishes, feelings of worthlessness, and so forth. When I have had similar feelings in a therapeutic hour with a patient, I have tended to be overactive. However, just as certain patients feel they must accept any comment the therapist makes in order to continue to receive love, many joke listeners feel the same anxiety when with a joke teller who may be insensitive and inept.

Humor always implies the presence of another person. As all dynamically oriented clinicians know, no drive exists outside the context of an object, and no understanding of object relations has much meaning unless we are aware of what drives are at work (Pine 1985). The teller of a joke narrates the anecdote or story and if successful motivates the listener to share emotionally forbidden thoughts and fantasies.

> The listener must share a delight in transgressing a prohi-
> bition. [He or she] must have a mind that can both be
> shocked and also illicitly pleased by the urges expressed in
> the joke. As regards the possible shock, he represents a
> superego which threatens the joke teller's underlying
> anxiety, that of unsuccessfully violating taboos. And as
> regards the possible pleasure, he must have an ego suffi-
> ciently integrated to admit to pleasures, even illicit ones.
> [Poland 1990, p. 215]

Although classical Freudians are sometimes accused of ne-glecting "object relations" in their diagnostic and therapeutic formulations, Freud (1905) emphasized "the object" or "the interpersonal" in his study of jokes and jokers. He viewed telling "dirty jokes" as similar to seducing a woman in the presence of a third person. He considered the joketeller as a first person and the listener as a third person. The listener "laughs as though he were the spectator of an act of sexual aggression" (p. 97), the seduced woman serving as the absent but implied second person.

Jokes and Psychosexual Development

Grotjahn (1957), Poland (1990), and Freud (1905) have all demonstrated that the development of a sense of humor parallels psychosexual development and the development of mature object relationships. From the infant's earliest smile (Spitz 1959) when orally gratified, through anal sadistic pleasure in manipulating others, to the excitement of playing with words in riddles and puns, and on to the aggressive and sexual jokes of teenagers, the line of development is determined by the maturing of drives as well as of object relations. What Poland (1990) calls "the gift of laughter," refers to the "relatively mature capacity to acknowledge urges and frustrations, hopes and disappointments, with a humor in which bitterness is tamed but not denied" (p. 199). This gift usually expands when the patient has undergone successful therapy.

Just as a mature sexual encounter recapitulates psychosexual development, so does a mature exchange of jokes. A fulfilling sexual encounter is usually initiated by words and kisses (oral), accumulations of tensions (anal), and consummation in penetration (genital). When the teller and listener are together and essentially loving, the mutual laughter that evolves from a joke can be similar to a mutual orgasm. In telling and listening to a joke, words (oral) lead to tensions (anal), which result in laughter (genital).

A psychosexual developmental perspective that includes, of course, a consideration of interpersonal relationships, can help us understand better certain features of the joke exchange. For example, there are certain individuals who never forget a joke and some others forget them quickly. There are many factors that account for this. First, if one is not made to feel too anxious by the oral, anal, or phallic-oedipal material in a joke, he or she will probably "take in" the material rather than reject it. Second, if one has positive feelings toward the joke teller, the possibility of remembering the joke will be stronger. Third, if one wants to "hold on" to the characters in the joke and/or symbiose with the teller of the joke, the joke will have a much better chance of being remembered than forgotten. Finally, if one likes to involve others in jokes, hearing one and planning to relate it to others strengthens the possibility of the joke being remembered.

When there are problems at different stages of psychosexual development, there will be barriers in the exchange of jokes. For example, certain jokers are so competitive with each other, constantly trying to top each other, that little mutual pleasure can take place between them. Some listeners feel raped, demeaned, and defiled by certain jokers and their jokes, and some of the latter may utilize jokes consciously and unconsciously to hurt or embarrass others. And just as there is the individual who can enjoy the same joke told over and over again by the same person, this may be compared to the mature lover who can enjoy making love over and over again with the same person and not be bored by it. In sum, the interpersonal satisfaction that can be derived from joke telling and listening is for some individuals similar to the mutual fun, excitement, empathy, and fulfillment that occur in good sex.

Mature humor, like mature sex, offers an opportunity for sustenance and consolation throughout life. It provides comfort without denying life's pains and aches (Poland 1990). According to Kris (1938) and Chasseguet-Smirgel (1988), the greatest accomplishment of humor is that it can banish the terror of loss of love. Its roots go back to the smile of the "infant at the breast when it is satisfied and satiated and lets go of the breast as it falls asleep" (Freud 1905, p. 146). As Chasseguet-Smirgel has said of the humorist, he or she "is trying to be his own loving mother" (p. 205).

It is hoped that the jokes that follow in the next several chapters, as well as their analyses, will provide "a soothing siren call away from attention to psychic horrors, loss of love and esteem, castration anxiety, death and nonbeing" (Poland 1990, p. 224).

2

You Can't Fuck Around with Love: Sexy Jokes

No dimension of human existence arouses more emotion than sexuality. Sex can provide intense excitement, bliss, and fulfillment, but it can also arouse powerful dread, depression, and guilt, as well. For many individuals, sexual impulses are something to conceal because to feel sexual excitement is to feel something forbidden. Inasmuch as many children are taught to deny their sexuality, they assume that their peers do the same. So, to talk about sex, to have sexual play, or to make love is something many people learn to believe requires manipulation and persuasion of others. I once asked a patient of mine how he felt during foreplay when he made love with his wife. He replied, "For me, foreplay consists of a half hour of begging!"

Enjoyable sex, like enjoyable joke telling, recapitulates psychosexual development. To kiss, hug, fondle, to be kissed, hugged, fondled, and eventually to have coitus assumes not only several conflict-free ego functions, but it also requires the acceptance of the child in oneself, as well as the child in one's partner. Not only is the freedom to regress necessary for enjoyable sex but one must have the ability to experience the partner as he or she is, rather than as a parental figure or reminder of a sibling. This is a tall order! Consequently, many individuals do not achieve sexual freedom. They find it very difficult to fuse tender and erotic impulses and be passionate with the one they love. Erica Jong, the novelist, confided through one of her characters in *Fear of Flying*, "The man I love, I cannot fuck. The man I fuck, I cannot love." Here, Jong poignantly and tersely describes the plight of many men and women. Unconsciously, these troubled individuals turn their sexual partners into familial figures; thus, they cannot permit themselves to feel erotic with them. The sex they have seems too much like incest. All of us have or experience this conflict and that's why there are many jokes that involve this familiar theme.

Sexual Inhibitions

Often is the erotic kept separate from the tender. In the *Oxford Dictionary of Quotations* (1992), love is defined as just a system for getting someone to call you darling after sex.

The title of this chapter comes from the story of the song-writer who was trying to peddle his song but was unsuccessful. He decided to consult a friend about the problem. The friend asked, "How are the lyrics?" "Better lyrics Ira Gershwin couldn't write," was the answer. "What about the tune, then?" his friend inquired. "A better tune Cole Porter couldn't write." "Well, what about the title?" the friend asked in trying to be helpful. The songwriter thought a minute and said, "Maybe it *is* the title." "What's the title?" The writer answers, "You Can't Fuck Around with Love."

The many jokes on sexuality seem to reflect the naïveté and perhaps ignorance that many people have regarding sexuality. They also reveal how much sex must be kept a secret and not a joy that is accepted with equanimity.

Sex starts at birth, if not before. If the infant is held, hugged, and fondled warmly and tenderly during the first year of life, he or she will probably be able to do the same with the sexual partner. However, many individuals remain fixated at the oral level of development and cannot move beyond being a baby in the sexual relationship. Either they suffered trauma during the first year of life or they have to regress to the oral period because higher levels of sexuality are too threatening to them.

> Mr. Klein came home very depressed. He told his wife he had just been to the doctor who said that if he didn't have human breast milk soon he would die. Mrs. Klein held him as he cried on her shoulder. "Don't worry," she said, "Mrs. Stein upstairs is nursing a baby. She'll help you." Mr. Klein found Mrs. Stein ready to help, and he suckled at her breast, which she found very stimulating. She asked Mr. Klein, "Is there something else you'd like?" Mr. Klein looked up at her and said, "Maybe you got a cookie?"

To remain sexually at the oral level like Mr. Klein is the fate of many individuals.

> Moe bumped into his friend John who said to him, "You don't look good. What's the trouble?" Moe sighed and answered, "Business is bad, my wife is no good, and the kids get on my nerves. I tried three therapists and not one of them helped me." "I've got just the answer for you," John said. "There's a woman up the street, you go up to her apartment, you take off your clothes. She puts a doughnut on your penis and she eats the doughnut slowly. You feel terrific!" Moe thought he might as well try this since nothing else seemed to help him feel better. A couple of weeks later, Moe runs into John who wants to know how it went with his recommendation. Moe tells him, "I did what you said. I went upstairs to the lady. I took off my clothes and she looked at me and said, 'Oh, a

Jewish boy!' and she took out a bagel, put on lox and cream cheese. It looked so good, I ate it myself."

Sometimes even oral gratification can arouse considerable anxiety.

Eleanor Roosevelt had a slice of pizza for the first time. She enjoyed it so much that she wanted to know how it was made. The owner took her to the chef who was patting the dough against his sweaty chest. She found that disgusting and said, "Oh I never would have guessed that is how you make pizza!" The chef retorted, "Lady, how do you think we make doughnuts?"

Anal Preoccupations

Many people cannot enjoy sex because they often equate it with urinary and anal functions. Children sometimes describe intercourse as "Daddy pees in Mommy's wee wee." Jokes that dwell on sexual themes are frequently called "dirty jokes" because they gratify anal fantasies. Oral and anal fantasies are sometimes combined such as in the following two jokes:

A drunk comes into a bar and says, "Shay, mishter, where's your men's room?" The bartender, annoyed that the man had bought his liquor elsewhere, says, "It's in the back." A moment later, the drunk returns and says, "It's locked." "Oh, yeah," says the bartender, "here's the key." The tilting drunk says, "A key? A key to your men's room? Why, my brother owned a bar for twenty years, he didn't have a key to his men's room, and he never had one piece of shit stolen!"

In a Spanish town, they are drinking beer in the local tavern when a man runs in and announces, "Gonzalez is in town!" whereupon everyone clears out, with the exception of one man who stays seated drinking his beer. The one who brought the news looks at him with surprise, "Don't you know Gonzalez?" The man replies with a smile, "Do I know Gonzalez? One day I was riding my horse and Gonzalez is riding his horse. Gonzalez sees me and takes out his gun and says to me, 'Dismount.' I dismount and Gonzalez tells me, 'Come to the back of my horse!' So I go to the back of his horse. Gonzalez says, 'Lift the tail!' so I lift the tail. Then he says, 'Kiss the horse' so I kiss the horse's ass. Then Gonzalez orders me, 'Eat the shit!' so I eat the shit. But then I say to Gonzalez, pointing my gun at him. 'Come to the back of my horse,' so he comes to the back of my horse. Then I say, 'Gonzalez, you lift the tail.' So he lifts the tail. Then I say, 'You kiss' and he kisses. Then I say to Gonzalez, 'You eat the shit' and he eats the shit. Do I know Gonzalez? We had lunch together!"

Genital sexuality seems so taboo to so many people that exclusive orality seems to be the only answer for them.

Jane meets her old friend Betty who says, "Jane, you look so terrific! Tell me, what's your secret?" Jane smiles demurely, and responds, "To tell you the truth, I'm having an affair." "Really," Betty comments. "Who's your caterer?"

Erik Erikson (1950) in *Childhood and Society* examines psychosexual development comprehensively. Like many other psychodynamic writers, he points out that to have satisfactory sexual relationships, one must have a satisfying oral period. This helps the individual not only to enjoy the closeness and intimacy of bodily contact, but to feel a trust in the partner and an inner certainty. Woody Allen's joking comments about his oral period may provide a clue to understanding some of his conflicted relationships with women. Said Allen on one occasion, "I was breast fed on falsies." Another time he confessed, "My mother never breast-fed me. She told me she liked me better as a friend."

Erikson (1950) postulated that the second year of life is a time when a child is helped to develop autonomy. If this is unsuccessful, he or she is full of doubts, obsesses a great deal, is ambivalent about many issues, and is full of guilt. Plagued by a punitive superego, this individual is either busily submitting to parental dictates or rebelling against them. This lack of autonomy, with its shame and doubt, inevitably invades the person's sex life in which he or she alternately rebels against internalized parental restraints and then arranges to get punished for transgressions.

> A minister was sermonizing on the Ten Commandments one Sunday morning in church. While preaching, he observed that one of his parishioners began to sob. A few moments later the same parishioner began to giggle. The minister was extremely puzzled and after church services asked about the mood changes. The parishioner responded, "When you talked about the commandment, 'Thou shalt not steal,' I realized that I did not have my $1,000 watch and I began to cry. A few minutes later you referred to the commandment, 'Thou shalt not commit adultery' and I remembered where I left it."

Talking about adultery, I once read in a discussion of the subject by a pastor, "Thou shalt not admit adultery."

Looking and Being Looked At

According to psychoanalytic theory, the oedipal conflict is extremely difficult to resolve (Fenichel 1945). Consequently, many individuals "look rather than touch" such as in voyeurism, or use their bodies to show off (exhibitionism) instead of making love and fulfilling oneself and one's partner. As we know, children are by nature peeping toms and some adults do stay fixated at this level.

A man was walking along a nude beach when he was confronted by a gorgeous, buxom blonde. He stared at her intently and then bellowed, "Wow, would you look good in a sweater!"

A story about Marilyn Monroe involves voyeurism, but I am not sure about its veracity.

Marilyn Monroe was lying naked under a sheet in a hospital room, about to go to surgery. One white-uniformed man after another lifted the sheet, looked, and walked off. After the fifth one, Miss Monroe asked, "Why are all you doctors looking at me?" The man answered, "Oh, we're not doctors, we're painters."

Most voyeurs are exhibitionists at heart and most exhibitionists in many ways are voyeurs. Often voyeurs and exhibitionists take turns being with each other, looking and being looked at. Leo Rosten (1985) tells the following story in his *Giant Book of Laughter.*

A shapely actress stepped out of the shower in her suite at a fine New York hotel, dried off, and stepped nude into her bedroom. A window washer outside her window was admiring her through the glass. She was so startled, she stood there nude and speechless. "What's the matter, sweetheart," said the window washer, "never seen a window washer before?"

Not only are psychotherapists voyeurs, but many physicians also have opportunites to satisfy and sublimate their curiosity as well.

The patient, Athelle St. Martin, was an extremely ravishing woman. Dr. Quinn greeted her, "Ms., or is it Mrs., St. Martin?" "Mrs. But I'm divorced twice," she responded. The physician requested, "Please take off your clothes and get on the examining table." Athelle blushed and said anxiously, "Doctor, please excuse me, I have this strong revulsion about undressing in front of anyone. Even with my husbands, I insisted they turn off the lights first." Dr. Quinn commented, "I'll be glad to turn off the lights. Just tell me when you are done." After a few minutes Athelle called, "All right, Doctor. Where shall I put my clothes?" Dr. Quinn responded, "Over here. On top of mine."

Phallic Exhibitionism

Men like to exhibit their virility. Often they can be more interested in receiving applause and adulation than in participating in a warm and tender sexual relationship. Woody Allen reminisced, "On our wedding night, my wife stopped in the middle of everything and gave me a standing ovation."

As men age, they feel more vulnerable and become extremely anxious about their sexual potency. Consequently, there are many jokes on aged men exhibiting their sexual prowess. I have observed that these jokes are very popular among those of us who are affectionately termed "golden agers." Exchanging them, we discharge some of our anxiety and occasionally receive some reassurance.

A man of 92 visited a house of prostitution. The madam indicated that she thought he was too old. He convinced her that he was capable by taking out his penis and ordering it, "Up, Caesar" and his penis became erect. "To the left, Caesar," he commanded, and his penis moved to the left. He bellowed, "To the right, Caesar," and his penis moved right. The madam was so impressed that she said, "I'm going to call the girls to show them." "Oh, no," responded the elderly gentleman, " I come to bury Caesar, not to praise him."

Saul Isaacs was placed in a home for the aged by his children, who thought he could not manage at home alone anymore. When he arrived, a lovely young nurse showed him to his room and suggested he take a shower before dinner. While he was in the shower, she came in and had sex with him. She told him he did not have to dress for dinner and just should put on his johnny robe . As he was shuffling along the corridor to dinner, he fell down, and before he knew it, a muscular male attendant jumped him and "shtupped" him. That night, his children came to see him, and he told them the day's occurrences. "Well, Dad," said his daughter, "you have to take the good with the bad." The old man said, "The good is that I have an erection once a year, but I fall on my face five times a day!"

Sometimes the anxiety about one's potency is so intense that exhibitionism can become a compulsion. The following two stories illustrate how certain men continually have to overcome their castration anxiety by reminding themselves and everyone else that, indeed, they do have a phallus that works!

Mr. Jacob Rabinowitz, age 79, visited a Roman Catholic church to make a confession. He told the priest that although he was a married man who had sex with his wife three times a week, he also had a 32-year-old mistress with whom he had sex three times a week. "I also have a former secretary I have sex with four times a week." The priest asked Mr. Rabinowitz if he was Catholic. "No," replied Rabinowitz. "Then why are you telling me this?" asked the priest. Jacob Rabinowitz announced, "I'm telling *everybody!*"

Receiving his annual medical checkup, Frank Connolly was asked, "How often do you have sex with your wife?" Connolly answered, "Twice a week." "Is that it?" asked the doctor. "Oh, no, I have sex with a girlfriend twice a week." As the doctor inquired further, Connolly reported "The maid twice a week. A neighbor twice a week." The doctor

admonished him, "You will have to take this matter in
hand!" Replied Connolly, "Twice a week."

An exhibitionist on the White House staff might have created
this one:

> One day President Nixon looked outside the window of
> the Oval Office and saw a message written in urine in the
> snow, "Nixon must go." Nixon ordered his aides to find
> the culprit and in a few hours one aide reported, "I have
> good news and bad, sir. We found the culprit, Mr.
> Kissinger, but the handwriting is your wife's."

Sometimes exhibitionists fail:

> An exhibitionist was flashing in the garment district of
> New York City. When he opened his coat, one woman
> designer responded, "Wow, what a lining!"

Sadistic Sex

Many individuals who feel vulnerable and weak can only enjoy
a sexual relationship if they turn their partner into an abused
victim. Cooperating with the partner is experienced as a form
of humiliating submission; consequently, sadistic individuals
are forever trying to get their partners to suffer, feel weak, and
become the powerless children that they themselves unconsciously feel they are (Strean 1983).

Many individuals utilize sex to hurt and frustrate their
partners in order to act out childish revenge on parental figures
and other family members. Because there is some sadism in all
of us (Klein 1957), we enjoy telling and hearing sexually sadistic
jokes. Some of our sadism is then gratified in a supportive,
nonpunitive atmosphere (Freud 1905) when we laugh instead
of feeling guilty.

Two teenagers were necking in the back seat of a car. As things heated up, Ron took Shirley's hand and put it on his penis. Shirley was indignant, saying to Ron, "How dare you do this. I don't do this kind of thing!" Ron was saying, "Could I just say one thing?" Shirley went on, "You are too crude. I won't go out with you again." Ron tried to inject a comment, but Shirley continued dressing him down. Ron said, "Couldn't I just say two words?" Shirley relented, and said, "What?" Ron said, "Let go."

A naked woman went into a church and sat down in a pew while the solemn service was being conducted. An usher came over and asked her to leave, but she insisted she had every right to be there. The usher finally grabbed her by the breast to pull her out of her seat. She yelled, "It's my divine right!" The usher said, "Your left is pretty good, too, but you have to go."

Dave and Fritz go on a hunting trip where Dave is attacked by a poisonous snake, which bites him on the penis. He is in pain and frightened, and Fritz runs to the nearby town to locate a doctor. The physician explains how to put his mouth over the wound, suck out the poison, and spit it out. That would be the only way to save Dave's life. Fritz returns to his friend, and in his pain, between gritted teeth, Dave asks, "What did the doctor say?" Fritz responds, "He said you are going to die."

A man walks into a bar and puts the crocodile he is carrying onto the bar. He zips open his fly, takes out his penis, puts it into the crocodile's mouth, and proceeds to punch the crocodile. He removes his penis, zips his fly, and says, "I'll give any man here ten dollars to do the same." A meek voice from the back responds, "I'll try, but don't punch me so hard."

Unconsciously we tend to associate sexual sadism with "the animal" in us. Coping with the animal in us, we often dream of animals who represent a part of our untamed id. Telling sadistic jokes that involve animals serves a similar purpose.

Betty Williams was on a safari, taking photos, when a big gorilla came down from a tree and carried her off to his lair. He abused her sexually in ways she had never even read about. While the gorilla was off eating a banana, a rescue party found her and took her to the hospital. When her friend Adele came to visit, Betty seemed very depressed even though Adele told her she was lucky to be alive. "Betty," asked Adele, "what's the matter?" Betty responded, "It's two weeks and he hasn't written or called."

An obese man went to a weight reduction clinc, and was asked to choose between the $100 and $200 treatment. He chose the less expensive one and was instructed to show up in the gym in shorts and sneakers. There, a gorgeous, naked woman had a sign on her that read, "If you catch me, you screw me." He chased her for an hour, and though he didn't catch her, he lost five pounds. He thought he might have better luck with the $200 treatment and at his next visit he chose that one. With eager anticipation, he came into the gym in his shorts and sneakers hoping to catch the woman this time. There he found a gorilla with a sign, "If I catch you, I screw you."

Charlie and George had been friends almost all of their lives. As their time on earth was drawing to a close, they made a pact that whoever died first would try to get in touch with the other. When Charlie died, George waited for a sign from his friend, and after a few months the phone rang. It was Charlie, and George wanted to know where he was and what he was doing. "Where I am, the grass is green, the air is clean. I get up in the morning, eat as much as I want, have a bowel movement, and make love. After a nap, I eat again and make love." George exclaimed, "You mean you're in heaven?" Charlie retorted, "What heaven? I'm a buffalo in Montana."

The War of the Sexes

In the process of growing up, no one is exempt from feeling envious. Boys envy girls and girls envy boys. (Of course we envy our own gender, too.) Envy does not cease at the end of childhood or adolescence; the competition between the sexes goes on at a feverish pace throughout life. We imperfect human beings always assume the grass is greener on the other side. Rivalry between the sexes is often expressed in sadistic language and action.

Jokes involving competitive sadism among men and women are many. As in almost all jokes, they gratify our hostile wishes without necessitating too much retribution. Here are some of the many sadistic stories that I have heard and told involving the battle of men and women. The first is a footnote from Rabbi Joseph Telushkin's (1992, p. 180) book *Jewish Humor*, regarding Golda Meir, Israel's former Prime Minister.

> Golda Meir's well-honed common sense, anger, and wit were not only directed against Israel's opponents. During the early years of the state, several rapes were reported to have been committed. At a cabinet meeting, one member proposed that women not be allowed to go out alone at night until the rapists were caught. "I don't understand the proposal," Golda Meir, the only woman in the cabinet, declared. "It's men who are committing the rapes. Men should not be allowed out at night."

So often do we believe, regardless of the tasks we have or don't have, that members of the opposite sex have it better.

> Alice Grant goes into labor and her husband takes her to the hospital. Throughout the night Mr. Grant hears her moans and groans from her room. He becomes very anxious, doubles his pacing, sweats like a pig, and has acute stomach cramps. Finally the doctor emerges, announcing, "You have a baby girl. Congratulations!"

"Thank God," says relieved Mr. Grant, "my daughter will never have to go through what I just did."

The battle between the sexes can continue until death.

Myron was on his deathbed, preparing to meet his Maker, when he smelled something delicious coming from his kitchen. He summoned his son and asked, as a last favor, to get him some of that delicious apple strudel he could smell. When the son returned, he said, "I'm sorry, Father, Mama is saving the strudel for after the funeral."

And even after death the sadism continues.

When Harry Cohen died, his wife called the *New York Times* to put in a death notice. She was told she had a choice of fifteen words for $100 or seven words for $50. She chose the seven word notice, and thought for a minute. "Harry Cohen is dead," she began. The clerk gently reminded her she had a total of seven words. Thinking again, she added, "Volvo for sale."

Sam's ashes were given to his wife in a container after the funeral. In private, she opened the container, said to Sam, "You always wanted a blow job," pursed her lips, and blew.

Ignoring Sex and Sexual Ignorance

Because sexuality activates many conflicts for many of us, our repressive mechanisms not only interfere with our enjoyment of sex, but we can become naïve and even ignorant about how to achieve a fulfilling sexual life. Sex therapy and sex manuals proliferate because many of us feel we just don't know how to do it and/or our partners do not have the finesse and sensitivity to satisfy us sexually.

There is so much repression of sexuality in our society even in our current age of sexual enlightenment, that there are many sexual anecdotes that focus on ignorance of sexual matters. Many of us derive much enjoyment from these jokes because they take care of at least two very important matters. First, the sexual ignorance belongs to the characters in the joke, not to us. Externalization and projection work for us at these times. Second, whenever a joke about ignorance is told, the real truth that is being held back by the ignoramus eventually emerges, so we get some free sexual information, all the time pretending we are knowledgeable, while we laugh at someone's stupidity. A pretty good deal!

> Mike visits his doctor, concerned because his penis is always purple. After a thorough physical exam, the doctor reports there are no organic dysfunctions. He asks the patient, "How often do you have intercourse?" Mike replies, "About three times a week." "Do you use contraception?" "Oh, yes," Mike informs him, "my girlfriend uses a diaphragm." The doctor inquires, "Does she use jelly?" "Yes," Mike answers. "What kind?" the doctor wants to know. Mike responds, "Grape."

Sexual naïveté is not confined to any one culture or ethnic group.

> A Scot, dressed in his native kilt, walks along the beach where he decides to take a nap. He stretches out and falls fast asleep. Three women walk by and comment that they always wondered what is worn under a kilt. Cautiously, without awakening him, they look and find out he wears nothing under the kilt. They decide to play a prank on him, and, searching through her pocketbook, one woman finds a piece of blue ribbon, which they tie on his penis. When the Scot awakens, he looks down and sees the blue ribbon. He says to his penis, "I don't know what ye've been doin' but whatever it was, ye've won first prize."

Often when we gratify our sexual wishes, we have to appease our superego. One way to do this is by pretending we are innocent.

> A few days before Christmas, Mrs. Spencer greeted the postman, invited him into the house, took him into the bedroom where she got undressed. She made love to him, and as he was about to leave, she handed him a dollar. The postman inquired, "You've been so nice to me, and now you're giving *me* a dollar?" "Well," Mrs. Spencer explained, "I'm doing what my husband told me. When I asked him what to give the postman for Christmas, he said, 'Fuck him, give him a dollar.'"

Ignorance of sexual matters is highest at puberty when sexual excitement is also at its highest and the taboos against it are at their most severe. The ego is simultaneously bombarded by strong id wishes and punitive superego commands. One way teenagers cope with this intense conflict is through lack of knowledge. I heard the following joke during World War II when I was about 12 years old.

> During a blackout in the middle of an air raid in England, a young teenaged girl ran out of the bomb shelter naked. She saw a young man about her own age riding a bicycle and asked if he could give her a ride home. "Sure," he said, "hop on and I'll drive you home." As the ride ended and she thanked the boy, she said, "I bet you didn't know I was naked." The young man responded, "I bet you didn't know this was a girl's bicycle!"

> A sexually inexperienced young man named Ira was about to get married. Totally unfamiliar with the facts of life, Ira asked his mother what to do on his wedding night. "When you go to your hotel room," she told him, "when your wife is undressed in bed, put your hand on her belly, rub gently around in circles, and say, 'I love you, I love you.'" Ira did

as his mother prescribed, gently rubbing his wife's belly and saying, "I love you, I love you." His bride became stimulated by this, and excitedly told him, "Lower, lower." Ira continued the same action, just lowering his voice three octaves and continuing to say, "I love you, I love you."

The lack of sophistication is such a popular defense against sexuality that it continues beyond the teenage years and into college.

The eminent psychoanalyst Bruno Bettelheim was teaching an advanced course in psychology and asked the class, "What is fellatio?" Since his question was greeted with a silence, he cajoled the class, "Come on class, what is fellatio?" Another silence. Finally, Bettelheim insisted, "One of you must know what fellatio is" and pointed to a coed. She responded with a quizzical look on her face, "I can't quite get it, it's on the tip of my tongue."

Another story about Bettelheim in the classroom was when he was teaching a class and found himself annoyed by the number of girls in the class knitting during the lecture. He made an interpretation, telling the females, "Knitting is a substitute for masturbation." The girls put their knitting away, and he happily went on with the lecture. At the next class, one student was knitting and he said to her, "Were you here last time?" "No," she replied. "Did you hear about my interpretation that knitting is a substitute for masturbation?" The student continued to knit, replying, "When I knit, I knit. When I masturbate, I masturbate."

Not acknowledging one's awareness of sexual matters remains a persistent defense. It also enters into marital relationships and serves as a protective measure for many spouses.

A married woman was asked if she smoked after sex. "I don't know," she replied, "I never looked."

A man was asked, "Do you talk to your wife after sex?" He answered, "It all depends. It depends if I'm near a telephone."

A couple is in bed and the wife says, "'arry, 'ow's about it?" Harry asks, "'ow's about whut?" "You know," she says. Nothing happens, and a few minutes later the wife says, "'arry, 'ow's about it?" Again Harry answers, "'ow's about whut?" and again the response, "You know." Finally, the wife demands, "'arry! 'ow's about it!" Harry again says, "'ow's about whut?" "'ow's about gettin' off!"

Although we are supposed to be living in an age of sexual enlightenment, the resurgence of the neurobiological approach to sexual behavior and its reinforcement by data from behavioral theories have tended to lead many people—therapists and non-therapists—away from the motivational approach of dynamic psychotherapy and toward a more mechanistic behaviorally oriented and social-engineered framework (Karasu and Socarides 1979). Thus, many adults, to enhance their sexual functioning, are poorly guided by uninformed sex therapists who prescribe bodily techniques of lovemaking (Kaplan 1974, Masters and Johnson 1970) rather than help people face their feelings and master their conflicts. When individuals naïvely focus exclusively on behavioral techniques to enjoy sex, the techniques usually backfire. There are many jokes that mock these behavioral techniques.

Morris was advised by his sex therapist to tell his wife Becky that if she would moan during lovemaking, he would be more potent. When they were making love that night, after a few moments, Becky asked, "Morris, shall I moan now?" "Not yet," Morris told her. Shortly Becky asked, "Shall I moan now?" and was told by Morris to wait. Finally, when Becky asked again whether she should moan yet, Morris said, "Yes, now." Becky took a deep breath and said, "Oi, vot a day!"

Frank constantly smoked cigars and his wife Marie hated the smell. He put out his last cigar of the day by the bedside at night, and first thing in the morning he lit one again. When Marie consulted a behavioral therapist about the problem, he suggested that she should put a cigar in her anus when she went to bed at night, and then put it by Frank's bed in the morning. Then, when he lit up, the taste would cause aversive conditioning. Marie tried this for two weeks, and when she saw the therapist, he asked her how the technique had worked. Marie explained that Frank had made faces, spit, and given up the cigars. The therapist was pleased until Marie continued, "But I have a problem, doctor. Now I can't fall asleep unless I have a cigar in my anus!"

Sex therapists have been very creative and inventive in trying to help men and women achieve more erotic satisfaction.

A group counselor from one of the Masters and Johnson classes suggested to two women that they go to a hotel with their husbands and stay in adjoining rooms. Each would give the other emotional support by her presence nearby and this might free both from their sexual inhibitions. On the first night, Mabel heard coming from Susie's room a series of noises, "Boom, boom, zoom, ah!" The next morning she asked Susie to explain the noises. "'Boom, boom' was when Sam approached the bed, 'zoom' was when he jumped through the air, and 'ah' was when he landed on me, and that was the most erotic satisfaction I ever had." Mabel said she would try the same procedure with Moe. The next night Susie heard, "Boom, boom, zoom, yowww!" and in the morning asked for an explanation. Mabel explained, "'Boom, boom' was when Moe approached the bed, 'zoom' was when he went through the air, and 'Yowww' was when he got his balls caught around the bedpost."

Very often there is so much confusion about sexuality that some individuals are never sure about what is permissible and what is not even when they are mature adults in other respects.

Joan and Jim were visiting friends and telling dirty jokes. Jim tried to get Joan to tell a joke he particularly liked but Joan was too shy to do so. Jim persisted and told Joan he would help her. "When it comes to the word 'shit' that you don't want to say, I'll spell it out," suggested Jim, and Joan agreed. Everyone was silent attentively waiting for Joan to tell the joke. Joan started the joke: "Well, there was this cocksucker . . ."

Every few minutes the nurse in Dr. Peterson's office would sneeze repeatedly, and she would breathe heavily. Dr. Peterson inquired what was happening to her and the nurse explained, "I have hay fever and every time I sneeze I have an orgasm." Dr. Peterson wondered, "What are you taking for it?" The nurse answered, "Ragweed."

As is true of most phenonema, what is sexually appropriate behavior and what is not varies to some extent from culture to culture. Rabbi Telushkin (1992) tells these amusing stories:

"How many positions are there for intercourse?" an instructor asks a university class on sexuality. "Seventy-eight," answers a French student, and proceeds to enumerate them. After he finishes, the instructor says, "But you didn't even include the most basic way, the woman lying on her back and the man on top of her." "Mon Dieu," the Frenchman exclaims, "Seventy-nine."

A Russian cosmonaut returns from outer space to his village in the coldest region of Siberia. The next day he is interviewed by Tass. "What is the first thing you did when you came back to your house and saw your wife?" "Better, comrade, if you asked me the second thing I did." "What was the second thing you did?" "I took off my skis." [p. 94]

Some people these days use the telephone to gratify their sexual desires. Individuals have been described as "giving good 'phone."

When Sadie Kerplansky's telephone rang, the elderly Jewish woman answered it, "Hello." The voice at the other end says, "You want me to come to your house and make passionate love to you. You want me to hold you close, to kiss your breasts." Sadie responds, "All this you know from one 'hello'?"

Sometimes those who are really knowledgeable about the physiology and psychology of sex are treated with disdain.

Perry went to his physician for his annual checkup. The doctor put Perry's urine specimen in a new machine that buzzed and hummed, and gave a readout that said Perry had tennis elbow. Perry was advised to return with a urine specimen in a week, and figured he could prove the machine was ridiculous. He put in urine from both his wife and daughter with some of his own sperm and presented it to the doctor. The machine again hummed and buzzed, and the doctor announced the results: "Your daughter is pregnant, your wife has syphilis, and Perry, if you don't stop jerking off, your tennis elbow will get worse."

A young woman walked into a sperm bank with her head tilted back, mouth full, and asked, "Where shall I put it?"

Alice's doctor told her to bring in a urine specimen. Instead, she arrived with a black eye and the doctor asked what happened. "I asked my friend Gloria what is a urine specimen. She said 'piss in your pot,' I said 'shit in your hat,' and we had a big fight!"

One of the most embarrassing experiences in the world for most people is to be observed having sex. It is as if one is caught committing a crime. In all probability the taboo against being seen having sex comes from the prohibition against viewing the primal scene. Just as children reason when they happen to see their parents having sex that something aggressive is going on, parents may feel that they are caught having a duel. Two true stories involving children observing sex between their parents have been told to me.

> I had a 6-year-old boy in treatment who told me that one night he walked in on his parents with Daddy on Mommy, and Daddy explained it was his way of "saying goodnight to Mommy."

> Some friends whose son was on our Little League team had the 9-year-old walk in on them during sex. Stu grabbed the sheet around him as he leaped off the bed, announced "We're playing Indian," and pranced around beating his hand against his lips doing an Indian dance, leaving his wife lying stark naked on the bed.

In a book *Outrageously Offensive Jokes*, Maude Thickett (1983) tells the following story:

> A horny pair of teenagers are driving down the highway; they can't keep their hands off one another. The young man, very aroused, says to his girlfriend, "Let's pull over and do it by the side of the road." "But people driving by will be able to see into the car," she protests. The boy pulls over on an incline off the highway. "Look, we'll get underneath the car, and I'll leave my feet sticking out. If anyone comes by, I'll tell him I'm fixing the muffler." Reluctantly, the girl agrees, so they wriggle underneath the car and start to make love. All of a sudden, the young man feels someone kicking his foot. "And just what do you

think you're doing?" a policeman asks. "Fixing my muf-
fler," the boy replies. "Well, you should have fixed your
brakes first because your car just rolled down the hill." [p.
86]

There are of course many "misconceptions" about pregnancy, so many that researchers now contend that the distortions about pregnancy are "inconceivable," and the issue may
be "unsurmountable."

> A saleswoman drove through a remote area in Mississippi
> when her car stopped functioning. Looking for help, she
> eventually walked to a farmhouse where two men were
> seated on the front porch. "How far is it to the nearest gas
> station?" "About 10 miles," answered one of the men.
> Then she asked, "Well, how far is it to the nearest motel?"
> "About forty miles," replied the other man. "Could you
> take me there?" she asked. "Don't have a car," is the reply.
> "Is it possible for me to stay here overnight?" is her next
> question, with the answer that she can, but she would
> have to sleep in the same bed with the men. The woman
> agreed, but before she got in bed, she handed each one a
> condom saying, "Please wear these so I won't become
> pregnant." She left the next morning when she got a hitch.
> Four months later, the two men are sitting on the porch
> when one says to the other, "Say, do you really care if that
> woman gets pregnant?" "No," he replies. "Then what do
> you think if we take these darn things off?"

As I recalled the above story, I began to reflect on some of my
own distortions about pregnancy when I was a child. Although
I used to love reading the medical books of my Uncle George,
who was an obstetrician and gynecologist, I thought "Labor"
was a town. We would be at my grandmother's on a Sunday
afternoon; the phone would ring, my uncle would answer it
and jump into his car saying, "I have a woman in labor."

A sexual pleasure that causes much conflict for many children, teenagers, and adults is masturbation. The Bible forbids it and so do the superegos of many nonreligious people. Masturbatory fantasies induce much guilt, and pleasuring oneself activates shame for many. The comedian George Carlin said, "If God had intended us not to masturbate, he would've made our arms shorter." And another comedian, Mike Binder, shared the following story: My father said, "Mike, if you masturbate, you'll go blind." I said "Dad, I'm over *here*!" I had a patient who told me the reason she felt guilty about masturbating was because she was "so bad at it." And capitalizing on one of the many distortions about masturbation, on my son's bulletin board was a cartoon in which a little boy was saying to his father, "Dad, if a girl masturbates a boy, which one of them goes blind?"

Distortions abound on sex, even in the classics.

> Little Red Riding Hood was walking through the woods when the Big Bad Wolf jumped out of the bushes and said, "Now I've got you and I'm going to eat you!" "Eat, eat," said Little Red Riding Hood, "doesn't anybody just fuck anymore?"

When I taught a course on sexuality in the master's program in social work at Rutgers, one of the students told this story to shed some light on how to lessen guilt over sexual matters:

> Mr. Bates opened up a brothel in a fancy hotel. To make it different from other houses of prostitution, he hired models, housewives, and teachers. Business thrived, but when his accountant reviewed income sources, he noted that most of the income came from the teachers. Mr. Bates decided to investigate. He listened at the doors of various rooms. At the rooms where the models worked, he heard, "Don't smear my lipstick." "Watch out, you're messing my hair." He realized why the models didn't do so well. From the housewives, he heard, "Pick up your trousers from the

floor." "Fold your tie carefully." The words coming from the teachers were, "You did that very well, but let's try it again so you can do it even better."

Sex and Manipulation

It is very difficult for many people to experience a sexual encounter as a mutually enhancing, cooperative venture between two equal partners. To be able to be empathetic without feeling masochistic, assertive without experiencing too much aggression, given to without worrying about being too dependent, and regressed without too much concern about being infantile takes a very "together" person. Many individuals feel used and abused when having sex and/or become preoccupied with how much they are using and abusing their partner. Instead of being enhanced, many men and women feel diminished by sex. A potentially cooperative venture can deteriorate into a miserable power struggle.

Inasmuch as many people view sexuality neurotically, they are very ready to believe that to participate in a sexual relationship requires the manipulation of and/or being manipulated by the partner. Thus there are many sexual jokes that contain the theme of manipulation. In telling and hearing these jokes, we can identify with the manipulating and manipulated characters but concomitantly feel apart from them as we mock them.

Even when men visit houses of prostitution, they can feel a compulsion to manipulate.

> Abe Horowitz from Israel visited "a house of horizontal refreshment" in New York. He asked the madam for a particular woman, Rena Schwartz, and was told she was the "top number" for whom the charge was $200 for the night. He said that was no problem, and spent an enjoyable night with her. The following night, Abe returned and again asked for Rena, replying to the warning about the fee

that it was no problem. On the third night, Abe repeats his visit, and in the morning Rena says to him, "You've spent three nights with me and I know nothing about you." "I'm Abe Horowitz from Israel." "Really," says Rena with pleasure, "my brother lives in Israel." Abe responds, "I know, he gave me $600 I should give to you."

Manipulation and persuasion are particularly used by teen-agers who usually have a great deal of ambivalence about sexuality. I recall telling the following joke many times in my high school years:

Sounds heard from a young girl's bedroom: "Oh, Johnny, please don't do that. Oh, Johnny, please . . . Oh, Johnny . . . Oh-h-h. . . ."

Very often one is interested sexually in an already-taken person, and wants to manipulate that desirable person's partner.

Tony approaches his friend Pasquale and tells him he would love to kiss Pasquale's wife Rosa's breasts. Pasquale is indignant, but Tony tells his friend he would make it worth his while, for, say, $200. When Pasquale discusses this with Rosa, she is also indignant, until hearing about the money, and she agrees to the arrangement. With much passion, Tony fondles, kisses, licks Rosa's breasts, all the time murmuring, "I don't know . . . I don't know . . . I don't know . . . " Finally Rosa asks Tony, "What do you mean when you keep saying 'I don't know'?" Tony responds, "I don't know where I am going to get the $200."

Attempts at sexual manipulation can lead to all kinds of consequences.

Tom enters a bar and sees a very attractive woman sitting at the end of the bar. He tells the bartender to give the woman a drink on him, and put some Spanish Fly in it. The bartender checks his stock and tells Tom that he's out of Spanish Fly but could put in Jewish Fly. Tom agrees to Jewish Fly, and the woman accepts and downs the drink. A few minutes later she sidles over to Tom and says passionately, "Take me, take me, take me shopping!"

I was told the next two stories during World War II.

A Nazi soldier seduces a young French woman, and announces after the sex, "In nine months is coming to you a baby! Heil Hitler!" The French lady responds in similar tones, "In three weeks is coming to you syphilis. Vive la France!"

A soldier who had been sexually abstinent for several months meets a WAC [Women's Army Corps] who has suffered from the same abstinence. The soldier blurts out, "So help me, I'll rape you!" The WAC replies, "So rape me, I'll help you!"

It is only within the last fifty years that our society has extended to women the right to enjoy sex. For many decades, women existed "to serve" and "to service" men. Fortunately, roles have shifted a great deal and at least in spirit men and women are both considered to be sexual persons. Although problems with sexual roles continue, we now see more examples of women attempting to manipulate men.

A golf pro was relaxing after a tournament in the country club's bar when he saw a lovely lass whom he befriended. After a few drinks and some warm conversation, they ended up in the golf pro's suite. After sex, the golf pro wanted to relax when his lady friend said, "Arnold Palmer was here last week and he had sex with me twice." Not wanting to be surpassed by Palmer, the pro went for a second round with the lady. No sooner was he trying to relax again when his sexual partner said, "When Jack Nicklaus was here we had sex three times." The pro pushed himself for another go, and felt exhausted, but the lady persisted, "Lee Trevino did it four times." The pro turned to the lady and asked, "What's par for this hole, anyhow?"

Sometimes it is difficult to know who is the manipulator and who is being manipulated.

In the courtroom the judge observed the very tall, muscled woman standing next to the small, emaciated man. He turned to the woman and skeptically inquired, "Do I understand that you are accusing this man of raping you?" "Yes, your Honor," was the confident reply. His Honor then asked the woman if the accused used a gun or tried any other type of force. The lady responded in the negative. The judge admonished the woman, "You are over 6 feet and weigh at least 200 pounds, where the accused is under 5 feet. I wonder how in the absence of a gun, and without force, rape could have taken place?" The woman responded, "I stooped a bit."

On a crowded bus, Mrs. Frank kept groping for her change purse in her handbag. A man in front of her said, "I'll pay your fare." Mrs. Frank declined and groped some more. Once more the man said, "I'll be happy to pay your fare." Again Mrs. Frank declined and tried to get her purse open. Finally the man declared impatiently, "Lady, you have already unzipped my pants three times."

We have reached the point in our civilization when men sometimes distort women's intentions.

Newlyweds Jerry and Jayne were having their apartment painted. As Jayne was getting out of the shower in the morning, she noted a handprint on the newly painted wall. She called to the painter and asked him to come up the stairs. Then she asked him, "Would you like to see where my husband put his hand in the dark last night?" The painter shyly responded, "I would, but first I've got to finish the downstairs closet."

Manipulative devices appear at times to be particularly inventive.

Lloyd met his friend Don and asked how he was. Don replied that he wasn't feeling well because he had a sore throat lasting several weeks. Lloyd commented that he had the same problem but he got rid of it. "How did you do that?" asked Don. "I'll tell you how," said Lloyd, "my wife gave me a blow job and it went away instantly." Don queried, "Is she home now?"

But trying to emulate a successful manipulator can sometimes backfire.

A gentleman was attaining much success one night picking up women at a bar. An inebriated fellow at the other end of the bar, observing the gentleman's achievements, was very impressed and asked him if he could confide how he attained his wonderful results. "I just smile and say 'Tickle your ass with a feather?' If the woman likes the idea, I'm her man. If she says, 'What?' or 'Pardon me,' I say, 'Particularly nasty weather,' and I go on to another woman." A little later the inebriated man wobbled up to a woman and asked, "Stick a feather up your ass?"

In Leo Rosten's (1968) *The Joys of Yiddish* he defined a *momzer* as "a clever or ingenious person, a resourceful, get-things-done, corner-cutting type" (p. 258). A *momzer* appears in this joke of Rosten's:

The *momzer* kept trying to persuade the woman to come to his apartment. She kept refusing. "Why not?" he per-

sisted. She said, "I'd hate myself in the morning." "So,"
the *momzer* suggested, "sleep late."

With so much anxiety and conflict surrounding sex, communication on the subject often goes awry.

Paul was having sex with his girlfriend in the back seat of
his car when a cop comes over and asks, "What do you
think you're doing?" Paul rolls down his window and
replies, "I'm screwing my girlfriend." "Good," says the
cop, "I'm next." "Sounds good to me," says Paul. "I've
never screwed a cop before."

Sex and the Elderly

As longevity increases by leaps and bounds, a great deal of
attention has been focused on the sex life of the senior citizen.
Most researchers on the subject (Karasu and Socarides 1979,
Strean 1983) have demonstrated that when the golden-ager is
unable to have sex, it is due more to psychological factors than
to anything else. However, many individuals continue to
believe that the senior citizen is a "has-been." I recall Dr.
Theodor Reik (1948) frequently making the remark, "When a
boy is 6, he thinks his penis is to urinate with. When he's 60, he
knows it." Although times have changed and the stereotype
has been modified, our culture tends to perpetuate the myth
that the senior citizen has "lost it."

One of the reasons our culture tends to disallow sex for the
elderly is that there seems to be an unconscious attempt on our
parts to stop parental figures from enjoying their sexuality. The
elderly, in turn, internalize the culture's biases and tend to
believe they are finished sexually. Consequently, most jokes on
the subject tend to reflect the senior citizen's empty sex life.

A group of elderly ladies started a canasta club. After a long discussion, the summary of rules for the club was given by the self-styled leader: "First, there will be no discussion of our grandchildren; we'll just bore each other. Second, no talk about vacations because we'll just be envious. Finally, let's not talk about sex; what was, was."

The elderly frequently like to recall "the good old days" and in doing so confess that it's been years since they've had sex. Said one senior citizen, "The last woman I was in was the Statue of Liberty."

When the senior citizen does discuss his or her actual sex life, it is difficult to determine what is fact and what is fantasy.

An elderly couple went to the doctor for their annual checkup. The wife stayed in the waiting room while her husband went into the office for his examination. During the examination, the doctor asked, "Mr. Stone, how is your sex life?" Stone answered, "The first time is great. But the second time, I sweat profusely." The doctor commented, "The second time, and you're 85 years old. That's wonderful." Then the doctor went into the waiting room and spoke to Mrs. Stone, "I was talking to your husband and he tells me the first time he has sex it is great, but the second time he starts to sweat a lot." Mrs. Stone responded, "He wouldn't lie to you. In January it's cold. In July, it's hot."

Inasmuch as there is such a peculiar mixture of truth and fiction in the stories the elderly present on their sex lives, jokes that deal with the subject reflect a wide range of practices.

Every night Charlie and Bessie, a couple in their late eighties go to bed together and every night Charlie places his hand firmly in Bessie's hand, they smile at each other for 2 minutes, and go to sleep. One night when Charlie started to place his hand in Bessie's, she stopped him saying, "Not tonight, I have a headache."

In contrast to Bessie and Charlie is the story of Max.

Eighty-four-year-old Max surprises his children by informing them he is marrying a 25-year-old woman. The children have many reservations, but Max will not listen. The children ask one of Max's friends to talk to him. The friend says to Max, "Your young wife might get a little bored. She probably should have some company her own age. Why don't you take in a boarder and when you are too tired, they can entertain each other." Max thinks it is a reasonable idea and some months later Max's friend calls to see how things are going. Max responds, "Things are great. My wife is pregnant." The friend says, "So you listened to me and brought in a boarder?" "Yes," answers Max, "She's pregnant too."

Many widows and widowers date and stories about their sexual practices abound.

Hannah, a widow of 82, met Cecil, a widower of 83. They dated and spent a lot of time talking about their pasts, their children, and their interests. They realized they had a lot in common and decided to get married. As they discussed their future with each other and were very frank about their likes and dislikes, Cecil finally asked, "How do you feel about sex?" Hannah replied, "Infrequently." Cecil asked, "Is that one word or two?"

Becky and Rachel, two widows, were comparing notes. Becky went first. "Every Wednesday night, Lou and I have an Early Bird, then we go to the movies. After that, we go back to my house where we hold hands and sing Jewish songs. How about you?" Rachel replied, "Every Wednesday, Ben and I have an Early Bird, and go to the movies.

Then we come back to my house, hold hands and then we fuck, because we don't know any Jewish songs."

Residents in a nursing home have all kinds of interpersonal interactions.

A man in a nursing home approached a woman resident there and said, "I bet you can't guess my age." She tried to put him off, but he persisted, and finally she said, "Okay, drop your pants." He did and she held onto his testicles a moment and said, "You're 92." Astonished by the lady's accuracy, he asked, "How did you know?" "Easy," she replied, "You told me yesterday."

An interest in sex can continue until death and may even become intensified as death becomes imminent.

Nat had not been feeling well so his wife Roz made an appointment for him to see the doctor. Later that day the doctor called Roz to tell her that Nat had less than 24 hours to live. Roz decided she would try her best to make Nat's last night the most wonderful night of his life. She prepared his favorite meal, with his favorite wine, and after dinner, put on her sexiest nightgown. "Whatever you want to do, we'll do." They made passionate love, and a few minutes later, Nat said, "Let's do it again" and they did. When Nat suggested a third time, Roz said, "That's easy for you to say. You don't have to get up in the morning!"

And the elderly still believe that sex is a cure-all.

Erna lay dying. Her husband Walter was at her bedside. As Erna seemed to be going downhill, Walter held her hand and asked, "What can I do for you?" Erna's eyes opened and she said, "Walter, one last time, let's make love." Walter protested, saying it would be bad for her health, but Erna would not back down. Walter reluctantly climbed on the bed and made love to Erna. To Walter's surprise, Erna seemed to feel better, with color coming into her cheeks, and she sat up in bed asking for a meal. Erna looked at Walter sitting by her bedside very dejectedly. "What's the matter? Aren't you happy? You've made me come alive." Walter sat with his head in his hands, "Just to think—I could have saved Eleanor Roosevelt."

Sex can be a rewarding experience. In fact, often it is given as a reward! I would like to end this chapter with one of my favorite jokes that suggests sex can be a rewarding experience.

There was a raffle at the local synagogue and the chairman was announcing the winners. "Third prize to Mr. Cohen, a 1994 Cadillac." The prize was accepted enthusiastically. Then, "Second prize, Mr. Levy, a chocolate cake." Mr. Levy indignantly shouted, "Vot's the matter! The third prize is a Cadillac. I get second prize, and you give me a chocolate cake?!" "But, Mr. Levy," the chairman pointed out, "the Rabbi's wife made the chocolate cake." "Screw the Rabbi's wife!" responded Mr. Levy. The chairman explained, "But that's the first prize."

3

Living in an
Institution:
Marriage

"Marriage is a great institution, providing you like to live in an institution," quipped Groucho Marx a quarter of a century ago. His notion that being married is similar to being imprisoned has been shared by countless numbers of philosophers, novelists, social scientists, and other knowledgeable commentators on the human scene. Groucho's sentiments are shared by no less a scholar than Voltaire, who referred to the state of matrimony as "the only adventure open to the cowardly"; by the novelist John O'Hara who wrote, "A married couple always presents an absurdly untruthful picture of the world, but it is a picture that the whole world finds convenient and a comfort"; by the anthropologist Ralph Linton who said that those who get married are suffering from a madness that is close to psychotic; and by the writer Oscar Wilde who suggested, "One should always be in love. That is the reason one should never marry." The Greek poet Palladas made an observation that has often been quoted: "Marriage brings a man only two happy days: the day he takes his bride to bed, and the day he lays her in her grave."

Although marriage or something akin to it has been an important institution in every known society, there has never been a Golden Age of Marriage gleaming at us from our history. From Adam and Eve to the present, there has been a mere handful of "love cultures" in which married people genuinely care for each other in a mature way whereby tender and erotic impulses are fused in a sustained, monogamous relationship (Fine 1979). Rather, since time immemorial, there has been "feuding, fussing, and fighting" by the majority of the wedded.

Even the Holy Bible has much to say against marriage. Paul advises his followers to refrain from marriage and to champion celibacy instead. St. Jerome opines that a man who ardently loves his wife is an adulterer. In the ancient kingdoms of Babylonia, Egypt, and Judea, subjugating wives was par for the course. When the ancient Romans stressed equality, the family broke up, and upon trying open marriage, the Greeks also helped, albeit unwittingly, to destroy many marriages (Ables 1977, DeBurger 1978, Grunebaum and Christ 1976, Strean 1985).

In attempting to refute the abysmal record that characterizes marriage throughout history, some writers refer to romantic love in twelfth century France and allude to the great lovers of history, such as Romeo and Juliet, Tristan and Isolde, Antony and Cleopatra, and Cyrano and Roxane. What is often overlooked in assessing these dyads is that all of the lovers lived apart from each other and had limited sex, if any. Romeo never saw Juliet in curlers and Juliet never had to ask Romeo to take out the garbage. Despite the defensive operations that sustained the Romeo–Juliet subsystem, Romeo's ambivalence was still apparent. Romeo described his libidinal cathexis toward his beloved as "a madness most discreet, a choking gall, a preserving sweet," something akin to sour milk! Although Romeo never met the philosopher Schopenhauer, the latter seemed to echo Romeo's sentiments about getting married. He described marriage as "the longing for an endless bliss with the possession of a definite woman, an unutterable pain that this possession is unattainable."

Despite the fact that the institution of marriage has provided much pain for many and much pleasure for only a small minority, marriage as an institution has never been rejected by any society. People go on getting married and often with high hopes for themselves. Although over the last century there has been a higher percentage of divorces than ever before in Western societies, there has also been a higher percentage of marriages. Marriage still continues to be a pervasive ideal (Stone 1992).

Considering the enormous ambivalence that married individuals have toward each other, it should not surprise us that jokes on marital conflict are in abundance. Almost all that are available, and they must number in the thousands, deal with the disappointments, dread, despair, and demoralization that husbands and wives experience. I have yet to hear a joke championing the institution of marriage, or one that deals with a married couple loving each other. Mutual hatred, power struggles, sex problems, divorce, and adultery are the major themes of the stories and anecdotes on marriage. They seem to reflect both our commitment to the institution and our wish to divorce ourselves from it.

There are many jokes in which the chief actor laments his marital state and wonders what caused him or her to make the horrible decision to wed.

> A patient told his therapist, "I never knew what happiness was until I got married — and then it was too late."

Parents who have suffered in marriage have all kinds of proscriptions and prescriptions for their children.

> A father said to his son, "You'll look at this day as the happiest day of your life." The son responded, "But, Dad,

I'm not getting married until tomorrow." "That's right, son."

A woman told her friend, "For eighteen years my husband and I were the happiest people in the world! Then we met."

A similar story goes like this:

Ray: "I've been married twenty-eight years today, and I'm still in love with the same woman." Jerry: "That's wonderful." Ray: "And if my wife finds out, she'll kill me."

From time to time individuals who have been married for many years are asked to comment on how they have been able to keep their marriage together.

Mr. and Mrs. Kevin McBride, in their early nineties, were celebrating their seventieth wedding anniversary, and a television crew from Belfast had come to interview them. "Now, then, McBroyde," said the interviewer, "siventy years is a mighty long toyme. In all those many years, did you never, even once, think of gettin' a divorce?" "Divorce? Me? From my darlin' Kathleen," blinked Mr. McBride. "Nay, man, not once!" The interviewer then turned to the wife, "And what about Mrs. McBroyde?" he asked. "Divorce? Never. Not once did the thought enter me mind," Mrs. McBride shrugged. "But, murder, ay, often!"

Even in our current age of scientific sophistication, psychological know-how, and equality of the sexes, violence among marital partners is pervasive. The battered wife now has a counterpart, the battered husband. In *Wife Beating: The Silent Crisis*, Langley and Levy (1977) reported that at least one-fifth of the married women in America beat their husbands, although few of the men admit it.

Because of the strong death wishes that spouses harbor

toward each other, many of the jokes on marriage are attempts to help people gratify their murderous fantasies toward the partner. One of Freud's favorite jokes was:

> A wife moving toward her golden years was planning her future and confided to a friend, "If one of us dies, I'm moving to Paris."

Not only are there wishes to kill the spouse during marriage, but vendettas occur even after the death of the partner. In Rosten's (1985) *Giant Book of Laughter*, he tells a joke that tends to demonstrate that "'til death do us part" is an incorrect notion. Revenge toward the spouse continues after death.

> Onto Phipps' Fine Foreign Cars lot drove a magnificent Silver Cloud Rolls Royce, out of which stepped a finely dressed woman, all in black. "I want to sell this car," she announced. The owner, Kenneth Phipps, glanced at the odometer (only 13,050 miles), got in the driver's seat, turned on the ignition, listened to the motor. "Uh, how much do you want for this car, madam?" "Fifty dollars." Mr. Phipps' jaw dropped. "What is this ma'am, a joke?" "No, just give me fifty dollars and a signed bill of sale." "Lady, are you out of your skull?" exclaimed Phipps. "Don't you know this Rolls is worth, even secondhand, thirty or forty *thousand* dollars?" "Yes, let's not waste time." "Madam, is this a stolen car?" asked Phipps. "Certainly not." "Is there a lien on it?" "Absolutely not. Now look, do you or don't you . . . " "Certainly I want to buy it. But fifty dollars. There must be a trick. Why would anyone in her right mind . . ." The woman in black arched an eyebrow. "I am entirely in my right mind, sir. I think you'll agree. You see, my husband just died. And in his will he stated that Flora Delago, who was his secretary—and his goddamn mistress—should get the full proceeds from the sale of his Silver Cloud Rolls Royce. Give me the fifty dollars." [p. 438]

Very frequently husbands and wives displace a great deal of their hostility toward each other onto members of the partner's family. The mother-in-law, for example, not only becomes the recipient of displaced hostility that belongs to her child, but in addition, mothers-in-law receive the hatred that their sons-in-law or daughters-in-law wanted to direct toward their own mothers, but were inhibited about doing so. Consequently, all in-laws, including sisters- and brothers-in-law, tend to be objects of destructive aggression before and after death.

Sue was dying and told her husband Mike that she had one wish she would like him to grant. The wish was that at her funeral, Mike should greet Sue's younger sister warmly and courteously. Mike protested, "I can't stand the bitch and I refuse." "Please, please," begged Sue as she lay dying, "one wish, one wish." Mike still objected, but as he saw Sue's breathing was becoming more faint, his guilt overcame him. So when Sue looked pleadingly at him, Mike said, "Okay, okay. I will say hello to the bitch. But it's going to ruin my whole day."

After Jeremiah Small's funeral, a gentleman who had been hired in advance, read what Jeremiah had written on how he wanted his estate to be administered. The proper speaking gentleman began, "To my wife Rose, two million dollars, my Cadillac, my Picasso, and everything in the store. To my daughter Jayne, an outstanding teacher, a graduate of Hunter, and a beautiful girl who doesn't find any man good enough, one million dollars. To my son Sidney, an excellent dentist, a fine golfer, one million dollars. To my brother-in-law Louis, who lived with us for thirty years, who never worked a day in his life, who smoked all of my fine cigars, and who said I would never remember him in my will, 'Hello, Louie!'"

A man visiting his wife's grave sees a man at a grave sobbing hysterically, "Why did you die? Why did you die?" The first man approaches and says, "I assume you are a relative of the deceased?" The man answers, "No, I'm not," but goes on crying, "Why did you die? Why did you die?" Somewhat puzzled, he asks, "Then who is the deceased?" "It's my wife's first husband."

When I have led workshops on the diagnosis and treatment of marital conflicts, I have enjoyed telling this story and then analyzing it with the therapists present.

A gentleman is at his wife's funeral and notices a man crying. He does not recognize the man and wonders who he is and why he is crying so intensely. At the grave site, the stranger cries even harder. Slowly it dawns on the gentleman that the man is his wife's lover. He goes over to the man, puts his arm around him, and says, "Don't feel so bad. I'll get married again."

In analyzing the manifest content of the above joke, mental health professionals have pretty much agreed on the following: The joke clearly suggests that every spouse has forbidden death wishes toward his or her partner because to be married takes a great deal of hard work and leads to much frustration. When sacred fantasies get punctured, we feel extremely angry and want to kill. So the setting of the joke, a wife's funeral, gratifies our forbidden wish to have our spouse dead.

Inasmuch as there is such a human but unconscious tendency to turn the spouse into a parental figure, many, perhaps most, sexual relationships in marriage are full of conflict. Many married people, without realizing it, are trying to be close sexually with a mother or father, and sometimes with a sister or brother. Hence, over 50 percent of married people feel much safer having sex with somebody who doesn't remind them of home and parents. The extramarital affair in the joke gratifies a wish in all married people to have a lover who is not a spouse.

Finally, nobody likes to be a victim. We hate it and fear it. To be a victim makes us feel weak, vulnerable, and impotent, that is, castrated. When one is married and has forbidden wishes to have extramarital affairs, these desires are often projected onto the spouse. "She'll cheat on me" is often easier to cope with than "I am a cheater." When a man projects onto the partner that she'll do what *I* want to do—have an affair—one starts to fear being a victim with all of the discomfort it conjures up for him. We laugh at the husband in the joke because he is the victim, not us, and when he's ready to be a victim a second time, what we fear becomes a little less ominous. We laugh, in part, out of relief, that he is the fool, not us. He is also controlling the situation to some extent, and we laugh *with* him because he arranges to be a little less of a victim.

Here is a joke that demonstrates how committed we are to the state of matrimony even with its pains and aches:

> Mr. Williams, a man in mourning, enters the office of his burial society. "I've come to make the funeral arrangements for my dear wife." "Your wife?" quizzes the society administrator. "But we buried her last year." "That was my first wife," sighs Mr. Williams. "I'm talking about my second wife." "Oh, your second wife. I didn't know you remarried. Congratulations!"

In order to appreciate better some of the latent meanings and unconscious purposes of jokes on marriage, it might be helpful to review certain other features of marriage.

On Choosing a Spouse

Most cultures idealize the institution of marriage. Pressure is placed on young and not so young people to find a mate. It is even a sin in certain religious groups to be unmarried.

Shirley was 33 years old and her mother was concerned that Shirley was still unmarried. Many attempts to "fix up" Shirley did not work out. Finally, Shirley's mother suggested she should advertise in the "personals" columns of a newpaper, and over Shirley's initial resistance, they made up the ad. "Young attractive woman, good cook and homemaker, looking for a fine gentleman." When the first response came, Shirley began to cry. Her mother pressed her, "What's the matter? You got an answer. What's wrong with that?" Shirley tearfully answered, "Mama, it's from Papa."

Advertisements do bring surprising responses.

A young man in his early thirties placed an advertisement in the newpaper, "Looking for a wife. Should be a good homemaker and a good mother." The gentleman received 110 replies. They were all from married men ready to hand over their wives to him.

Although it is not as common a practice today, many prospective grooms still ask their intended fathers-in-law for their daughter's hand in marriage.

The young man said to his girlfriend's father, "I'd like your daughter for a wife." The reply was, "Bring over your wife and I'll see if I want to trade her for my daughter."

Matchmaker Stories

In Eastern Europe, the professional matchmakers, *shadchen* in Yiddish, traveled from village to village trying to locate eligible young men and women so that they could "make a match." As he or she gathered data about potential mates, the complementary factors in their personalities and way of life of their families were assessed. The fee was based on consummation of a marriage; consequently, he or she was a shrewd salesperson. As mentioned previously, Freud was very fond of *shadchen* stories. Here are some of the ones he particularly liked.

Shloime Zanger, having attentively listened to Shadchen Markowitz's sales pitch, said, "But in all the wonderful things you told me about the girl, you left out one important thing." "Me, never," Shadchen Markowitz protested. "What did I leave out?" "She limps," said Zanger. "Oh," shrugged the *shadchen*, "Only when she walks!"

Oscar Stavsky, a *shadchen*, after having been extremely laudatory about a female client, brought the interested young man to meet her. The young man looked her over and tersely said, "Glad to meet you," obviously very dissatisfied. "What's wrong?" the *shadchen* asked. In a low voice, the young man said, "You told me she was young, and she's over 40! You said she was attractive, and she looks like a chicken! You said she was . . ." The *shadchen* interrupted, "You don't need to whisper. She's hard of hearing too."

Morris Silverman confronted the *shadchen* and said in anger, "You lied to me!" "Me? Lie? Never!" answered the *shadchen*. "Isn't she pretty? Well educated? Loves the arts?" "Yes, yes," Morris replied, "but you also said she comes from a famous family. You said her father is dead—and I just found out he's in jail." Retorted the *shadchen*, "That you call living?"

Joe Bernstein, a *shadchen*, was praising the charms of Judith Schwartzkoff to Bernie Kozinsky, a confirmed bachelor. "Judith?" said Bernie, "she's almost blind!" "That you call a failing?" cried the *shadchen*. "That's a blessing— because she won't see what you are doing." "But," said Bernie, "she also stutters." Sighed the *shadchen*, "You are lucky. A woman who stutters doesn't dare talk too much, so, she'll let you live in peace." "But she's also deaf," complained Bernie. Bernstein replied, "I should have such luck! To a deaf wife you can shout—you can bawl her out!" Bernie still complained, "She's at least twenty years older than I am." Snapped the *shadchen*, "I thought you were a man of vision. I bring you a wonderful woman, a woman you can spend a lifetime with, and you pick on one little fault."

As the reader can easily see, every *shadchen* joke and all of the stories we have told about choosing a mate imply that marriage is hell! Veterans of marriage are disgusted, prospective wives and husbands are cynical, and this is why a *shadchen* emerges as something of a psychopath. He's trying to make something potentially disastrous appear positive and we laugh at his antics, secretly knowing that marital bliss is an illusion. Why is happiness in marriage often elusive and illusive?

Falling in Love

The ancient Roman philosophers described falling in love as a form of madness. *Amare et sapere deis non conceditur*—the ability to keep one's wits when in love is not granted even to the gods. Many centuries later, another philosopher, George Santayana, in obvious agreement with his profession's predecessors, described the process of falling in love and wanting to marry as that "deep and dumb instinctive affinity." In *Marriage and Morals*, another philosopher, Bertrand Russell (1929), pointed out that falling in love and getting married occur when people realize that they have finally found a means of escape from the loneliness that afflicts them throughout their lives. It should be noted, however, that for Russell the extinction of his loneliness through marriage did not endure for long. He was married four times!

In consonance with virtually every commentator on the falling in love process, all of whom view it as a highly irrational, illogical, and childish state of affairs, Carl Jung (see in Evans 1964), believed that the search for a mate was completely unconscious. "You see that girl . . . and instantly you get the seizure; you are caught. And afterward you may discover it was a mistake."

Freud (1939) likened romantic lovers to fond parents who project their own ideals onto their children in order to substitute for the lost narcissism of their childhood. Reuben Fine (1985), an eminent authority on love and its vicissitudes, has pointed out that being in love has very many unrealistic qualities, is obsessional, and egocentric. In agreement with Freud, Fine has emphasized that the loved one is made into a perfect parental figure and becomes the recipient of fantasies that emanate from the lover's childhood.

One of the reasons that most married individuals have to cope with much unhappiness is that they feel very deprived. Having overidealized the partner and having expected to see childhood and paradise restored in a Garden of Eden of Marriage, they are extremely disillusioned. As the demands of living intrude, each partner gives less and demands more. It is the coincidence of giving less and expecting more that punctures the romantic ideal and sparks many conflicts between spouses (Ables 1977). The plight of many newlyweds has been well illustrated by Arthur Miller (1964). In the play *After the Fall*, Miller has the wife say "If you really loved me, you would do much more." The husband answers, "No one loves that much, except maybe God."

Inasmuch as most marital partners have a powerful tendency to turn the spouse into a mother and/or father, many marital problems emerge. As we saw in Chapter 2, when the spouse is unconsciously turned into a parental figure, sex can be experienced as if it were forbidden incest.

Two good friends, Barry and Ed, were having a reunion. Each had gotten married during the past year and were comparing notes. Ed asked, "You know the best way to

stop a woman from wanting sex?" "No, tell me," says
Barry. "Marry her," was Ed's reply.

Perhaps it was the spouse of Ed or Barry who was written up
in a newspaper item: "The bride stood in the deceiving line."
Those of us who do marital counseling observe consistently
that husbands and wives have a strong tendency to displace a
great deal of the sadism that is unconsciously felt toward their
parents onto their marital partners. Some spouses will even
deceive themselves into believing that their marital partners are
nothing but very cruel and depriving people, and that their
parents are and have been nothing but nurturing and loving
souls.

> It was two minutes before midnight on a cold, snowy
> night. The temperature was ten below zero. Scantily
> dressed, Mr. Samuels enters a bakery that is about to close,
> and in a barely audible voice asks for two small rolls. The
> storekeeper asks, "What else?" "That's all," says Mr.
> Samuels. "My God," exclaims the storekeeper. "It's mid-
> night, it's cold as hell, and you come out for just two small
> rolls! Did your wife send you out on a night like this?" Mr.
> Samuels answers, "Who do you think sent me out, my
> mother?"

We laugh at Mr. Samuels because he behaves like a frightened little boy who has turned his wife into a hostile and
controlling mother. His own mother, in his mind (and probably
only in his) is a sweetie pie! We mock Samuels because we are
familiar with his plight but do not want to confront the Mr.
Samuels in ourselves. Long before Freud, it was clearly ac-
knowledged that when a young man gets married, he divorces
his mother.
Inasmuch as the institution of marriage is frequently utilized
as an arena to reenact childhood conflicts, the marital partner
inevitably becomes the object of the spouse's chronic complaints. I have come to the conclusion that every chronic

marital complaint is an unconscious wish. Show me the husband who constantly says, "My wife is a cold, frigid bitch," and I'll show you that the man unconsciously desires such a wife. A warm, responsive wife would frighten him. Similarly, show me the wife who constantly says, "My husband is a weak, passive schmo," and I'll show you the woman unconsciously desires such a man. A strong, active husband would scare her.

In 1521, King Henry VIII asked an interesting rhetorical question that has never been fully answered, "Who does not tremble when he considers how to deal with a wife?" Subjects of Henry VIII, to keep track of the extensive list of his royal mates (he had six wives), counted them off in a little refrain: "Divorced, beheaded, died; divorced, beheaded, survived" (Fraser 1993).

Even before one gets married, the problems of commitment are somewhat recognized.

> Sherman told his friend that he was getting married and his friend asked, "Have you picked a date yet?" Sherman responded, "Wow, I didn't know you could bring a date to your own wedding!"

Commitment to a marital partner is a very anxiety-provoking experience for many people. During the last two decades we have observed many couples who live together but vow never to get married. And, when some of them do get married, they fight day and night. Marriage makes them feel like entrapped children. Psychologically, these individuals are back home again and experience the marital partner as a restrictive parent.

> Question: What do you call a woman who knows where her husband is twenty-four hours a day, seven days a week? Answer: A widow.

Power Struggles

Another of Groucho Marx's quips was, "Marriage makes strange bedfellows." The main reason for this is that we all tend to recapitulate our childhoods in our marital relationships. Since husbands and wives are often in a regressed state as they relate to their marital partners and therefore feel some of the emotions of a child, such as the primitive dependency, intense anxiety, and powerful obligations, they often feel weak and vulnerable. As clinicians know, when anyone feels weak and vulnerable, there is a strong tendency to demean, derogate, and deride others. This is what many marital arguments are about. Two individuals who feel weak and vulnerable are trying to weaken the other through endless power struggles. In *Who's Afraid of Virginia Woolf?*, a couple argues every day and every night for twenty years. But they are children in many ways and can't bear leaving each other because they need each other too much.

> Mrs. Donovan began to hit her milquetoast of a husband with a bat. He kept running away from her, fleeing from her blows finally by crawling under the bed. "Come out of there, Patrick, you coward!" she yelled. "No," Patrick shouted, "I'll show you who is the boss in this house."

Husbands particularly must deny their feelings of vulnerability and passivity.

> While Elizabeth and Trevor were lying in bed, two big, brawny men entered the house and came into the bedroom. One of them drew a circle with chalk on the floor and told Trevor to stand in the circle and not to leave it. The two men took turns raping Elizabeth, and then left. Elizabeth screamed at Trevor, "You didn't say a word. You didn't do a thing. You could have dashed to the phone.

> Damn you! You just stood there!" "Oh no," said Trevor. "I
> fooled them. When they weren't looking, I took a few steps
> out of the circle."

Because husbands and wives are basically children with each
other, and therefore are intimidated by each other, they are
frequently trying to cover their tracks.

> When Doug left to play golf in the morning, he promised
> his wife Jean that he would be home well before their
> dinner guests arrived so he could help. He played nine
> holes and, despite his golf partners' objections, he ex-
> plained that he really must leave. On the way home, on an
> isolated road, he saw a woman standing by her stalled car.
> He got out to help her, and it took a long time for him to
> figure out and correct the problem. The attractive woman
> was very grateful, and apologetic that because of her he
> was all greasy. She insisted that he should stop at her place
> to wash up. One thing led to another and they ended up in
> bed, spending so much time that Doug arrived home later
> than he had promised his wife he would be there. He
> decided to tell his irate wife the truth. After listening to his
> story, Jean sneered at Doug and said, "You're a damned
> liar. You played 36 holes!"

Even when marital partners seem to be kind and giving
toward each other, latent hostility can emerge.

> Max goes into a very expensive stationery store and tells
> the salesman that he would like to buy the finest Mont-
> blanc pen the store has. Max tells him, "It'll be a present for
> my wife's fortieth birthday." "Oh, I bet she'll be sur-
> prised," says the salesman. Max says, "I'm sure she will.
> She's expecting a mink coat."

When spouses do accept gifts from their partners, often they
are not pleased. Rabbi Telushkin (1992) in a section on "Materialism" tells this story:

A sexy young woman walks into a dinner party on the arm of a much older man. At the dinner, the lady sitting next to the woman says to her, "That's a beautiful diamond you are wearing. In fact, I think it's the most beautiful diamond I've ever seen." "Thank you," the woman replies, "this is the Plotnick Diamond." "A diamond with a name," the lady says, "how romantic! Is there a story behind it?" "Oh yes, this diamond even comes with a curse." "A curse?" asks the lady, "what's the curse?" "Mr. Plotnick." [p. 75]

Money and other forms of materialism are often considered to be the root of all the evils in marriage.

Said Nick to his friend, "They say I married my wife because her uncle left her a whole lot of money. That's not true. I would have married her no matter who left her the money."

Marvin turned to his wife Florence and said, "Dearie, tomorrow is our twenty-fifth wedding anniversary, so why don't you go and pick out a real nice new mink coat for yourself." "Thank you, Marvin, but I don't want a nice new mink coat." "Okay, Flo, how about a diamond necklace?" queried Marvin. "No," replied Florence, "I already have a diamond necklace." "Then how about a new Cadillac?" "Stop, stop, I don't want a car," Florence responded with annoyance. Marvin then beseeched, "What *do* you want, Florence?" "What I want," said Florence, "is a divorce." "A divorce? Gosh, Florence, that I can't afford!"

As marriage goes on and the partners age, they both become more sensitive about their appearance and their physical functioning.

Mr. Green came home to find his wife sitting naked in front of the mirror, admiring her breasts. "What do you think you're doing?" he asked. "I went to the doctor today

and he said I have the breasts of a 25-year-old," replied
Mrs. Green. "Oh yeah?" replied Green disparagingly,
"and what did he say about your 55-year-old ass?" "Nothing," responded Mrs. Green, "your name didn't come up
at all."

The comedian Joe Laurie, Jr. liked to tell this story.

> Shirley was out driving with her husband. She was
> speeding along at about fifty. Suddenly a motorcycle cop
> appeared alongside and told her to pull over. The cop
> looked at her and said, "I'm going to put you down for
> fifty-five." Shirley turned to her husband and sneered,
> "See, I told you this hat makes me look too old!"

Spouses can be quite sadistic in demeaning the partner's
looks and appearance. Unconsciously they know that for most
people to degrade appearance punctures narcissism and this is
what they are trying to do.

> A wife looks at her husband one evening and asks, "Do
> you think I'll lose my looks when I get old?" The husband
> answers, "If you are lucky."

As clinicians have long recognized, when two individuals
want to fight, they can use anything to fight about (and if two
individuals want to get along, they can find many areas of
agreement). Spouses who feel childish and vulnerable much of
the time can even fight about the weather.

Myron Cohen, the well-known comedian of the 1950s, told
this one:

> Sam and Rebecca are in bed one night, and she wakes up
> and says, "Sam, get up and close the window. It's cold
> outside." Sam just keeps on snoring. A little while later
> Rebecca nudges Sam again saying, "Sam, get up and close
> the window. It's cold outside." Sam awakens but tries to

go back to sleep, but his wife keeps shaking him, so he finally gets up and shuts the window. Back in bed, he says, "So, now it's warm outside?"

Asexual Marriage

As we discussed in Chapter 2, because making love is an interpersonal experience, if husband and wife harbor hatred toward each other, they will argue about who is to blame for their mutually dissatisfying sex life. That is why many psycho-therapists have recognized that to help a marital dyad enhance their sex life, the spouses' hateful feelings toward each other have to be modified—not the sexual techniques utilized. Inasmuch as making enjoyable love requires two individuals to love each other, sexual difficulties in marriage are rampant. Therefore we find many jokes on how husbands and wives displease each other sexually.

> Ernie asked his wife, "How come you never tell me when you are having an orgasm?" His wife answers, "Ernie, you're not around."

> A patient complained to his therapist, "My wife insists on turning off the lights when we make love. That doesn't bother me. It's the hiding that seems so cruel."

> Stated another patient after her divorce, "I think that's what we fought the most about—our sex life. I wanted one."

Although farmers are close to nature, they are not exempt from sexual difficulties.

> Farmer Bill Smith was drunk again. "You know, Annabelle," he said to his long-suffering wife, "if you could only lay eggs, we could get rid of all those smelly chickens."

Annabelle did not reply, so Farmer Smith tried again. "You know, if you could give milk, we could get rid of that expensive herd of cows." Annabelle finally responded, "You know, Bill, if only you could get it up we could get rid of your brother Bob."

Both rich and poor, when married, suffer from enormous sexual anxieties and inhibitions.

The late Aristotle Onassis suffered from chronic impotence. One day he left his villa in Greece for a consultation with a physician in London. After a thorough examination, Onassis was told that before having sex with Jacqueline Kennedy, his wife at the time, he should knock his penis on the bedpost, which will give him a long-lasting erection. Onassis thought the recommendation worth trying, and prepared to leave the doctor's office. The doctor confided, "This is an excellent treatment. I prescribed it for Wilt Chamberlain and he's now considered an outstanding lover. He's rumored to have had sex with thousands of women." Onassis became very optimistic, got into his plane, and arrived very late at his villa. Jacqueline was sleeping when he arrived, so in the dark he whipped out his penis and knocked it on the bedpost a few times. Jackie, awakening, cried out, "Is that you, Wilt?"

Sexual anxieties and inhibitions in marriage exist in virtually every culture and ethnic group.

On the night prior to her daughter's marriage, a French mother was giving the daughter advice. "Annette, if you want your marriage to be a good one, never go to bed in the nude. Your husband will find you much more interesting if you make yourself a little mysterious. He will be much more intrigued and stimulated if you *never* go to bed naked." Two weeks went by and Annette's husband became troubled and asked, "Is there some insanity in your family?" Annette answers, "Definitely not! But why do you ask?" The husband says, "Well, we are now married two weeks and every night you go to bed with that damn hat on your head."

Resolving Marital Conflicts

Because conflict in marriage is pervasive, there are many "marriage savers" (Koch and Koch, 1976) in the marketplace using a diversity of treatment modalities and subscribing to a variety of theoretical perspectives. There are numerous stories on marital counseling that usually mock the process, the expert, and the client.

A man had received three years of intensive marriage counseling. He reported to his wife, "Darling, I got a wonderful insight. I learned that I'm constantly talking about myself. This has to change! You talk about me."

During the course of marriage counseling, spouses make many confessions.

Norman told his wife after four years of twice-a-week marriage counseling, "Rena, I realize you think I'm too nosy." "Bravo," said Rena enthusiastically, "how do you know?" Norman replied, "I read it in your diary."

Robert Newcomb went to see a therapist because his life was humdrum. He felt particularly apathetic in his marriage; everything had become routine for him. The therapist asked Robert to describe a typical day in his life. Robert complied and in a characteristic monotone, said, "I get up at 6:00 A.M. I drink my orange juice and then eat my prunes. Then I bathe and shave." As Robert continued obsessively recounting the day's events, the therapist became quite drowsy and struggled to keep himself awake. Nonetheless, Robert droned on, talking about getting dressed, taking the subway, etc. In order to keep himself alert and with the hope that he might give Robert a psychological shake, the therapist advised, "Mr. Newcomb, there is not enough spontaneity in your life. When you get home tonight, I want you to grab your wife as soon as you see her, throw her on the floor, and make love to her right then and there. See me in three days." Three days later at the therapist's office, when Robert was asked how things were going, he responded, "I did what you told me. As soon as I came home, I took my wife, placed her on the floor, and made love." "How was it?" the therapist wanted to know. Robert, in his monotone, replied, "It was humdrum for me but the kids liked it."

A marriage in the 1990s is probably more difficult to sustain than ever before because role requirements for husbands and wives are in transition. The rights, privileges, and immunities of both men and women are constantly being challenged and questioned. As a consequence, women often seek out other women who become their "sisters" and men do likewise with men. Often the "brothers" and "sisters" carry on like sibling rivals.

Three married women who were in a consciousness-raising group together agreed to the three couples going on a vacation together. However, the women made their husbands agree in advance that there would be no golf. Although the "brothers" agreed to their wives' request, they could not resist the attractive golf course and made a reservation for the next morning at 7:00 A.M. They also planned that each of them would have to find a way to renege on his promise to his wife. All three men were on the first tee at 7:00 the next morning and the first man asked, "How did you get out of your promise?" "I promised her a diamond necklace." "Wow," responded the first man, "I had to promise her a Jaguar." Then they both turned to the third husband to ask, "What did it cost you?" "Nothing," he answered, "I woke her up at 2:00 A.M. and asked, 'Intercourse or golf course?' and she answered, 'It's chilly in the morning. Take a sweater.'"

Group therapy for the treatment of marital problems has become quite popular.

A group leader was going around the room asking each member about the frequency of sexual relations with marital partners. When he asked, "Once or more a day?" a few hands went up. "Once or more per week?" and a few more hands went up. Gradually everyone in the group was covered except one man. He didn't raise his hand to "once a month?" or "once every two months?" Finally, the leader got to "once a year?" and the man waved his hand very enthusiastically. The leader was puzzled and asked, "How come you are so excited? Once a year?" The man continued waving his hand enthusiastically and shouted, "Tonight's the night!"

In the same group, a member made an interesting confession. "This morning my wife gave me a definite promise of maybe."

Very often clergy assume the role of marriage counselor.

A wife was telling her rabbi that her husband had many limitations. Whatever she complained about, the rabbi said, "You're right!" The woman left the office feeling better. Then her husband came in and complained about his wife. Again the rabbi uttered, "You're right. You're right." The husband left feeling a bit better. As the rabbi left his study, his wife sneered at him, "I overheard you. First you told the wife she's right about everything! Then you tell the husband he's right about everything! They can't both be right. You're a fake, a charlatan . . . " The rabbi responded, "You're right!"

Priests also do marriage counseling. Sometimes it is used conjointly with confession.

> Wayne was talking to his priest and said, "I gave up sex for
> Lent. Well, at least I tried to, but the last day of Lent my
> wife dropped a can of peaches and when she bent over to
> pick it up, I couldn't help it." The priest said, "That's
> understandable. A lot of people cannot resist sexual temp-
> tation." Wayne then asked, "You are not going to dismiss
> us from the church?" The priest said he would not do that.
> "Thank God," Wayne exclaimed, "They threw us out of
> the supermarket."

Husbands and wives often save some of their contemptuous
remarks to embarrass each other in public.

> Jason and Marie Smith played weekly bridge with the
> Martins. Jason and Marie constantly bickered with each
> other and usually lost to the Martins. During one intense
> game, Jason had to get up in the middle of the game to go
> to the bathroom. While he was gone, Marie said to the
> Martins, "This is the first time I know what's in his hand."

Dynamics of the Extramarital Affair

A very common means of adapting to marriage in the 1990s is
by having extramarital affairs. Inasmuch as there are many
jokes on the vicissitudes of affairs, it will be helpful to examine
some of the dynamics of the affair.

Many clinicians, perhaps most, agree with anthropologist
Margaret Mead (1967) who contends that monogamous hetero-
sexual love is probably one of the most difficult, complex, and
demanding of human relationships. Marriage challenges our
mature ego functions—frustration tolerance, impulse control,
acceptance of reality, empathy with others, and so on. These
are demands that most married individuals resent in an age of
sexual freedom and narcissism. Thus, many individuals seek
escape from marriage.

The percentage of married people engaged in prolonged

extramarital affairs keeps rising, with the current rate about 60 percent for married men and over 40 percent for married women (Strean 1985). In an extramarital affair, the individual in effect has two part-time mates, both of whom are important to him or her. To those involved in these "open marriages" (O'Neill and O'Neill 1972), one intimate, monogamous relationship feels frightening, demanding, frustrating, or boring.

Those who have researched the extramarital affair (Bartusis 1978, Block 1978, Hunt 1969, Strean 1980) have demonstrated that husbands and wives involved in affairs are unhappy people who "need" their affairs for one or more reasons. They may be escaping from an overwhelming fear of a symbiosis, they may be running away from a parental figure who appears like a punitive superego and seems too controlling, or they may be trying to seek reassurance regarding their sexual identity. A very common reason for an affair is an unresolved oedipal conflict (Dicks 1967, Eisenstein 1956, Strean 1980). When the marital partner is ascribed the role of parent, sex takes on incestuous connotations and has to be avoided. Many men experience their wives as "virgin mothers" who must be avoided sexually while they turn their girlfriends into "whores" who excite them. Although these men rationalize their sexual inhibitions, dissatisfactions, and frequent impotence with their wives, they unconsciously feel they are little boys with big mothers. The same may be said for many women who unconsciously turn their husbands into fathers (and/or mothers), and must avoid them sexually and seek another partner.

Despite the ubiquity of the extramarital affair, the responses of the "injured partner" can be quite extreme when he or she learns that the mate has been involved extramaritally. Murderous or suicidal feelings, deep depression, and revengeful fantasies are fairly common. Some "injured partners" respond with cold indifference or curiosity. A few are fascinated and can even show exultation. Very few "injured partners" are ready to acknowledge how they have unconsciously colluded in the affair and subtly sanctioned it.

Because of the many conflicts that an extramarital affair expresses, there are numerous jokes on the subject. The jokes reflect many of the dynamic issues just discussed.

Apparently marital infidelity was known during biblical times.

> Moses comes down from Mount Sinai with the Ten Commandments. "I have good news and bad news," he tells his flock. "The good news is I got them down to ten. The bad news is, adultery is still one of them."

One of the issues that is frequently discussed regarding an extramarital affair is the tremendous denial utilized by the injured party. Many clinicians have noted that husband and wife can both be involved extramaritally for years and neither party is consciously aware of the other's activities. It is such a narcissistic injury to know that one's marital partner is involved in an affair that suspicions and doubts are frequently repressed. Isaac Bashevis Singer, the well-known writer, enjoyed telling the following classic (Telushkin 1992):

> A gentleman, concerned about his wife's fidelity, goes away on a business trip. Before he leaves, he tells his son, "Watch everything your mother does and give me a complete report when I return." When he comes back and asks his son, "Did Mommy do anything unusual while I was away?" the son tells him, "The night after you left a strange man came to the house. He kissed Mommy on the lips when he came in, and they hugged for a long time." "And then?" the man asks. "Mommy took him into the bedroom." "And then?" "I looked through the keyhole. He took off his pants and shirt and then his underwear." "And then?" "He started to take off all of Mommy's clothes and he was kissing her the whole time." "And then?" "Then Mommy turned off the light and I couldn't see anything." "God in Heaven," the man said, slapping himself. "These doubts will kill me!" [p. 97]

Extramarital affairs just don't happen. They are sought.

> Charlotte, a married woman in her forties, was bored with her married and family life in the suburbs. One day she asked her friend Laura for some confidential advice. "Laura," she blushed, "how do you go about having an affair in this town?" Laura responded, "I always start with the Star Spangled Banner."

Learning about the spouse's affair arouses deep emotional conflict. Therefore, there are many jokes that relate to this theme.

> Tim Flannery came home early and to his shock and surprise he saw his wife Maggie under the sheets with his best friend Patrick. "Maggie," cried out Tim, "Me own wife! Me own true love." How kin ye be doin' such a terrible thing. And you, Pat, me best friend. . . . Hey, Patrick, can't ye even stop while I'm talkin'?"

> Tony asks Luigi, "Luigi, do you like a woman with a big, big belly, or a small belly?" "Small belly," Luigi answers. "Luigi, do you like a woman with a big, big ass, or a nice small ass?" "Small ass." "Luigi, do you like a woman with big, big tits or nice, round tits ?" "Nice round tits," answers Luigi. Tony asks, "Then Luigi, why you fuck my wife?"

Occasionally a spouse will ask a friend for advice when he or she suspects the marital partner of infidelity. Leo Rosten (1985) in *Giant Book of Laughter* tells this amusing story:

> Two women were sharing confidences over their tea. "I don't know what to do about my husband anymore," said Louise. "Do you know that he never comes home until long past midnight?" "Oh dear, my husband used to be like that—but no more." "What changed him?" Louise wanted to know. "What changed him, my dear, is that every time he stealthily opened the door at one or two or

three in the morning, I would sweetly call out, 'Is that you, Everett?'" "That was all there was to it?" "Uh huh." "But why would that stop him?" "Because his name is Harold." [p. 242]

Sometimes spouses project their own wishes for extramarital affairs onto others.

"Judy," said Kay, "we've been friends for years and . . . " "What are you trying to find out, Kay?" "Look, I don't want to be improper or out of line, but . . . " mumbled Kay. "Look, you can ask me anything; we're good friends," Judy reassured Kay. "All right, " Kay said after a deep breath, "Judy, are you cheating on your husband?" Judy shrugged, "On who else?"

When Woody Allen's affair with Mia Farrow's daughter became known, many criticized him. In part the criticism was a way of deflecting some of our own wishes to do what he did. Maude Thickett (1983) tells the following story:

An Italian couple are spending their wedding night at the house of the bride's parents. Rosa sits on the bed as her husband undresses. He takes off his shirt and she sees the thick hair covering his chest. Terribly upset, she runs downstairs to her mother. "Mama," she screams, "he's got hair all over his chest like an animal." "Calm down," says her mother, "and go back upstairs. It's your wifely duty." Up she goes, just in time to see her husband remove his trousers. Again the bride bolts from the room and runs to her mother. "Mama, he's got hair all over his legs like a monkey!" "Silly girl, go back upstairs and make love to your husband like a good Italian wife." Once again she returns to the bedroom to find her husband removing his shoes and sees he has only half a left foot. "Mama," she runs screaming downstairs, "he has a foot and a half." Her mother pushes her aside, "Stupid girl! You stay down here and *I'll* go upstairs." [pp. 78–79]

Infidelity is even discussed in heaven.

> St. Peter is interviewing three men who have arrived at
> heaven's gate. He asked the first fellow, "How did you get
> here?" The fellow replies, "Well, I live in this tall apartment
> building and one night when I came home I suspected my
> wife of cheating on me. We got into a big fight and I got so
> mad I picked up the refrigerator, pushed it out the window
> and had a heart attack." St. Peter asked the second man
> how he got to heaven. "I was in my convertible in front of
> this apartment building and a refrigerator fell on my
> head." St. Peter asked the third fellow his story, and was
> told, "I don't know. I was sitting in this refrigerator . . . "

Because many husbands and wives fantasy having affairs,
they are always ready to be accused of it even if they haven't
acted on the fantasy. Rosten (1985) relates this story, which
took place in Paris:

> Michelle Fauver, a pretty painting model, skipped up the
> stairs to the studio of Jacques Benoit, for whom she was
> posing in the nude. She entered the atelier with a bright,
> "Bonjour, Monsieur Benoit." "Bonjour, Michelle," he
> sighed. "No, no, cherie, don't undress. I'm not feeling up
> to snuff this morning. I don't feel like working. Sit down.
> Let's have some coffee. We'll get back to the painting
> tomorrow." They were having coffee, chatting about in-
> consequential matters when Benoit suddenly froze. Foot-
> steps were heard coming up the stairs. The painter lis-
> tened, slammed down his cup, and said, "My wife!
> Michelle, quick—take off your clothes." [p. 38]

As we suggested in our earlier discussion, responses vary
considerably when one finds out that the marital partner is
having sex with someone else.

> Al walked into his bedroom and saw his wife making love
> with his good friend Jim. Al said, "Jimmy, I have to, but
> not you?"

The infidelity fantasy can be too strong.

> Frederick Springham, a Southern plantation owner, phoned his mansion and his butler answered. "Hello, how are you?" asked Mr. Springham. "Ahm jest fine," was the reply. "Everything all right at home?" "Ah-uh—giss so, suh." Mr. Springham became irritated and asked, "What do you mean, you guess so? Anything wrong with my wife?" "No, suh, she ain't sick . . . " "Then put her on the phone." There was a long silence. Mr. Springham became more irritated and said, "I'm telling you to put my wife on the phone." The butler answered, "Well, suh, that's jest it. Your wife is in the bedroom—but she ain't alone." "What?" Mr. Springham said irately. The butler then informed Mr. Springham that she was in bed with "the man from Atlanta." Springham was raging and began giving directions to the butler. "Go into my study. There's a gun in the top drawer of my desk. Take the gun and shoot both the man and my wife." Springham warned that he was coming right away and if the butler didn't follow his directions he would be fired. Mr. Springham said, "Now go do what I told you to do. I'll wait on the phone until I get the report." In about 4 or 5 minutes, the butler returned to the phone and said, "Okay, Ah did what you tole me to do." Mr. Springham asked, "Did you shoot them both?" "Yas, suh. Ah was so nervous. Ah ran to the back garden, and ah threw the gun in the swimmin' pool, and now . . ." "Swimming pool? We don't have a swimming pool . . . Listen, is this Cloverdale six four two one?"

Just as there is a range of reactions when a husband or wife learns of the partner having an affair, there is a rich diversity of responses when one is caught in the act.

> Werner Blackman, a rather unsophisticated gentleman, arrived home early one afternoon to find his wife and best friend in bed. "Oh my God," cried out Werner. "What are

you two doing?" His wife turned to her lover and said, "See, didn't I tell you he knew from nothing?"

At the beginning of this chapter I suggested that rarely do we find a joke on marriage where the theme of love is present. The following story comes close.

The waves were high and pounding the beach. The lifeguard pulled the limp Abraham Cohen out of the water as a crowd gathered around them. "Get back," the lifeguard bellowed. People blurted out, "Get a doctor!" "Give him air!" "Go get his wife!" The lifeguard yelled out again, "Stand back, I'm going to give him artificial respiration." "You are not," cried out Mrs. Cohen, pushing her way through the crowd. "My Abie gets real respiration or nothing!"

We also pointed out at the beginning of the chapter that despite the growing divorce rate, people also go on getting married in increasing numbers. With longevity helping the phenomenon we now meet individuals who have been married two, three, four, five, and six times and we consider most of them relatively sane.

A dapper, elderly gentleman was walking alone along a street. He heard footsteps behind him and felt a little alarmed. He slowed his pace, and the footsteps slowed. He quickened his steps, and the footsteps speeded up too. He realized he would have to deal with the problem and wheeled around to see an elderly woman following him. "You are following me, going faster when I did, going slower when I did," he accused her. She agreed saying, "You remind me of my third husband." "Third husband, how many times have you been married?" the man demanded. With a demure smile, the lady said, "Two."

Despite the many pains, agonies, and frustrations of marriage, those who have suffered in it still praise it. Bertrand

Russell (1929) pointed out that the yearning for a loving relationship with a mate is never extinguished even in old age. William Shakespeare, who experienced severe marital conflict, said in Sonnet 116:

> Let me not to the marriage of true minds
> Admit impediments. Love is not love
> Which alters when it alteration finds,
> Or bends with the remover to remove.
> Oh no! It is an ever-fixed mark
> That looks on tempests and is never shaken.

4

Loving and Hating Parents, Hating and Loving Children: The Parent–Child Relationship

It is only within this past century that children have been regarded as unique specimens. It is also a relatively novel concept that parents have a responsibility to provide their offspring with consistent tenderness, love, and care. Historians such as Lloyd DeMause (1982) who have examined the history of childhood have documented centuries of violence and infanticide dating back to biblical times. The advice "Spare the rod and spoil the child" was stated and illustrated many times in the Bible.

From ancient Rome to colonial America, children have been struck with rods, switches, and canes. They have been whipped, castrated, and destroyed by parents, often with the consent of political and religious institutions. To beat the devil out of a child was a mandate to provide salvation for the child who had been corrupted by original sin. The further back in history we go, the lower is the level of child care, and the more likely it is that children were killed, abandoned, beaten, terrorized, and sexually abused. The history of childhood can be described as a "nightmare" (DeMause 1982).

Until the early 1900s children were supposed to exist largely, if not exclusively, to satisfy parental wishes. As many a parent will still say, "I expect my child to give me pleasure and if the child doesn't, I feel furious." Although this notion might seem farfetched to the sophisticated 1990s man or woman, go to any Little League baseball game and watch parental violence as the mothers and fathers exploit their children so the parents can feel like winners (Strean and Freeman 1991).

It is only recently that children are being regarded as children, not as little adults who live to gratify their parents' narcissism. Although it is a relatively new notion, parents, teachers, and others who live and work with children are now realizing that youngsters cannot act like little adults. Children need much time and encouragement to learn the demands of reality. They are entitled to make mistakes as even mature adults are permitted to do.

Those of us who have worked clinically with parents and children in child guidance clincs, family agencies, mental health centers, and in private practice agree that parents tend to condemn in children the behavior they cannot tolerate in themselves. When adults cannot accept their own yearnings for dependency, wishes to rebel against rules and regulations, and sexual and aggressive fantasies, they are very much inclined to be intolerant of children who by their very nature constantly express these feelings and sensations. Everything adults have felt as evil in themselves may be projected onto children. This is why, over the centuries, children have been considered devils, tied up, swaddled, and tortured. Adults have believed children must be restrained and in doing so have denied what they feel are their own wicked wishes (DeMause 1982, Strean 1979).

Psychotherapy with children and their parents mirrors what has transpired in the outer culture. Originally the child guidance movement was conceptualized as one in which the child was the complete focus of diagnostic and treatment attention; the therapist devoted all of his or her efforts to understanding and alleviating the child's intrapsychic conflicts. Until the late 1930s the parents' contribution to the child's therapy was to present to the therapist the child's problems and history as they saw them and then be relegated to the waiting room for the duration of the child's treatment.

By the 1940s with the aid of psychoanalytic theory, child guidance workers began to realize that a child had unconscious meaning to parents, and their own anxieties and fantasies influenced the growth and development of the child. Professionals learned that a childhood behavior disorder or neurosis was often, if not always, unconsciously induced and sustained by the parent, and therapeutic modifications in the child's behavior, no matter how positive, adversely affected the parents' equilibrium (Sternbach 1947). First mothers were made clients and their participation in the treatment process helped the child's therapy. When the mother's wishes, fears, and neurotic conflicts were addressed, the child's therapeutic gains did not threaten her so much. However, as mother and child improved in their internal functioning and modified their transactions with each other, the father often felt excluded and became threatened by their changes (Beron 1944, Burgum 1942).

Although it took much longer for child guidance personnel to help fathers become clients of child guidance clinics, by the mid-1960s many fathers were actively participating in their children's treatment (Grunebaum 1962, Grunebaum and Strean 1970, Strean 1962). A natural step in the evolution of the child guidance movement was the realization that the family could be viewed as a social system with interdependent parts, and a change in one part of the system could alter the entire system.

As psychotherapists in the 1990s, regardless of our theoretical orientation or preference of modality, we all endorse the importance of the parent–child relationship in the growth and development of the human being. We also recognize that because all human specimens—adults and children—are vulnerable organisms with many sensitivities, idiosyncrasies, and anxieties, conflict (intrapsychic and interpersonal) is inevitable. Consequently, to help parents and children cope with the frustration and despair, the agony and terror that exist for all of them some of the time, jokes about parents and their children proliferate. I have examined hundreds of these jokes, and many have a common theme—the narcissism of the parents. Let us deal with this subject first and then review some of the jokes on parental narcissism.

Parental Narcissism

Most therapists agree that the wish to have a child is an expression of one's narcissism. For most parents, a child represents themselves reproduced and it is frequently observed that parents endow their infant with traits that they pride or wish for in themselves. Those parts of themselves that they love or wish to possess are frequently perceived in the child, and that is why the child is often experienced as "His Majesty the Prince" (Freud 1914).

The dynamics of narcissism are observed in the proud and oft-repeated statement of parents and grandparents that the child "looks like me." When negative attributes are perceived by parents, it is not uncommon for one to blame the other for causing them or to claim that the focus of the difficulties is in the genetic history of the other parent. The narcissistic element in parenthood has become quite clear when one views parental reactions to children's report cards, or their artistic or other accomplishments. "That's my son!" "That's my daughter!" are only thinly veiled exclamations that really imply, "Look how great I am!" Similarly, it is difficult for many parents to acknowledge psychological difficulties in their children because unconsciously this means acknowledging difficulties, limitations, and vulnerabilities in themselves.

Parents love to show off their children's birth, and there is a lucrative industry in printing birth announcements. Through these announcements, parents can exhibit their sexual prowess and fertility. They can also reveal their narcissistic ideals by sending out "Mr. and Mrs. Martin Silverstein proudly announce the birth of their first son, Dr. Lawrence Silverstein."

That children are used to exhibit one's sexual competency can be inferred by the anxiety and embarrassment that one notes occasionally around announcing the adoption of a child. And the double meaning in kidding about artificial insemination, "Spare the rod and spoil the child," shows some of the anxiety attached to it.

Mothers and fathers want their children to project a perfect image of the parents. How a child appears to the world sometimes seems of more importance to their parents than what a child actually feels. "Look nice!" is a frequent parental admonition because otherwise the family name may be disgraced.

> A new grandmother is wheeling her granddaughter in a carriage. A friend stops her and says, "What a beautiful baby girl." "Oh," responds the proud grandmother, "you should see her pictures!"

I remember becoming very much aware of the strength of parental narcissism in the 1960s during the primaries for the presidential election. For many years on Friday nights I called my paternal grandmother who lived in Canada. I did this for at least two reasons. First, my father had predeceased her, so that hearing from me reduced some of her grief. Second, I derived a great deal of succor and wisdom from my grandmother. It was May, 1968, when my grandmother was in her late eighties, that we were debating the merits of the respective candidates. She was very much for Robert Kennedy while I preferred someone else at the time, and in the heat of our debate I asked, "So why do you want Robert Kennedy to be President of the

United States?" She replied, "It would make his mother very happy."

Parents frequently impose their own expectations onto their children without sufficient consideration of how the young-sters are emotionally affected. This is particularly true about the offspring's choice of vocation or profession.

> As Mrs. Caplansky was pushing a pram with two little boys in it, she met a friend. "Good morning, Mrs. Caplan-sky. Such darling little boys. So, how old are they?" "The doctor," said Mrs. Caplansky, "is 3, and the lawyer is 2."

My grandmother is involved in another story about profes-sional choices. I come from a family that has doctors, dentists, and lawyers. Thus there was enormous pressure on me to get a doctorate, and partly because of this pressure I kept post-poning studying for it. Finally after many years and much hard work, I got my degree and was so eager to report my accom-plishment to my grandmother that I called her from Columbia University right after defending my dissertation. "Grandma," I said excitedly, "I got my doctorate!" "Good," she replied, "maybe now you'll go to medical school."

I believe grandparents feel less ambivalence toward their grandchildren than they felt toward their own children. The grandparent does not live with the child, so does not have to deal with the day-to-day conflicts, frustrations, and responsi-bilities. Because of the age and status of grandparents, they tend to be more idealized. In any event, the love that a grandparent has toward the child as well as the devotion shown are often intense.

> Grandma was with her grandson Joey at the beach when he walked into the water. Before she could do or say anything, a powerful wave swept Joey underwater. Grandma became extremely terrified and beseeched, "Dear God, please, please, bring my Joey back! God, my

one and only Joey! I'll do anything, God, if you'll bring him
back!" Seconds later Joey was deposited at her feet. She
looked him over and with great relief saw that he was alive
and well. "God," she called, "Joey had a sailor hat on.
Where is it!"

As the child grows and develops, parents brag about the
youngster to relatives and friends.

Three women are bragging to each other about their
respective sons. The first mother says, "My son is so
considerate. Do you know he bought me a Cadillac?"
"That's nothing," says the second woman, "my son paid
for me to have a trip to Europe." The third mother chimed
in, "That's nothing compared to my son. He goes to a
psychotherapist four times a week. He pays one hundred
dollars an hour and he speaks about nothing but me."

The competition among parents and grandparents is strong
and persistent.

One grandmother said to her two friends, "My grandson
graduated from Harvard, went to Yale Medical School,
and is now a resident at Mt. Sinai Hospital." The second
grandmother commented, "I'm proud of my grandson. He
was Phi Beta Kappa at Princeton, was on the Law Review
at Columbia University, and now he's a famous district
attorney." The third grandmother said, "I'm extremely
proud of my grandson. He came out of the closet and
courageously announced that he's gay. He's living with
two nice boys—a resident at Mt. Sinai Hospital and a
famous district attorney."

Jackie Mason (1987), the comedian and commentator on
social institutions has discussed narcissism in Jewish parents
from many vantage points. Mason asks, "Did you ever see

what happens if a Jew has a son who drives a truck? If you know such a Jew, say, 'Does your son drive a truck?' 'Drive? I wouldn't say he drives it. He sits in the truck. I wouldn't say he drives it. How would it look, a truck moving with nobody there? In case it gets out of control, he controls it. He's not driving—he's controlling it—that's it! He's a controller in the trucking business'" (p. 73).

Changing a son's or daughter's job title to enhance the parent's status is not confined to Jews. A friend of mine whose son opened a barber shop told me his son was "a tonsorial artist." A garbage collector was called "a sanitary engineer" by his mother. A father spoke of his daughter being a "social director" when she was running a house of prostitution. Many parents whose offspring are social workers will think up many titles other than "social worker" when they talk about them to friends. Through their children, parents try to be the biggest and the best.

> Five fathers were bragging about the size of their respec-
> tive families. Said the first: "I've got four sons; one more
> and I'd have a basketball team." The second responded,
> "So I have five sons; one more and I'd have a hockey
> team." The third topped them with, "I have eight sons;
> one more and I'd have a baseball team." The fourth father
> announced," I have ten sons; one more and I'd have a
> football team." "Sit down all you guys," admonished the
> fifth father. "I have seventeen daughters; one more and I'd
> have a golf course!"

Parental narcissism is never fully gratified.

Parental Frustrations

Parenting, it seems, involves coping with many frustrations. Many expectations that parents have for their children go unfulfilled and this inevitably arouses much anger and intense frustration in the parents. In addition, parents have to face other difficulties. It is a finding of dynamic psychology that all parents recapitulate their own childhoods as their youngsters traverse the psychosexual stages of maturational development. For example, when a mother is breast-feeding her infant, she is also reliving unconsciously her early life as an infant, and experiencing the emotions and conflicts that she experienced during her oral period. The same can be said when toilet training a youngster, and on through life. One of the main reasons it is difficult being a parent is because parents not only have the realistic problems and challenges of rearing and nurturing their youngsters but they have to deal concomitantly with their own unresolved issues from childhood. This is usually a big demand on most parents.

Because the parents' inability to cope with a child's maturational conflicts is so intimately related to the parents' dynamics, those of us who work clinically with children and their parents have come upon a very useful formula. What a parent presents as a child's problem is really the parent's unresolved maturational task. For example, a therapist can recognize that the statement, "My child doesn't respond to limits," reflects anxiety in the parent that interferes with limiting the child. As the clinician interviews this parent, she or he will look for clues that pinpoint why the parent unconsciously does *not* want the child to respond to limits. Similarly when a parent says, "My child needs sexual information," it can be inferred that it is the parent who is probably in need of such information (Despert 1965, A. Freud 1965).

Because being parents induces many hardships that activate resentment and revenge in them, there are numerous jokes that deal with the frustrations and irritations of being a parent.

The comedian Sam Levenson (1979) who often reflected on the pain and anguish of raising children suggested, "Insanity is hereditary. You can get it from your children." If parents don't

go crazy from their children, at least they can be driven to
drink.

> Two women leave their children home for a few days and
> check into a hotel. Prior to having dinner, one of the
> women invites the other to join her at the bar for a drink.
> "I never drink," her friend responds. "Why not?" she is
> asked. The nondrinker says, "In front of my children I do
> not think it is right to drink, and when I am away from the
> children, who needs to?"

Although parents praise their children, reinforce their
strengths, and support them through hard times, the parents'
resentment comes through. A colleague of mine told me that
his mother frequently told him that he could do anything he set
his mind to do when he grew up. One day she asked him what
he would like to do professionally and the son said he would
like to be an opera singer. Retorted his mother, "With your
voice?"

> Two old friends meet and one says, "I haven't seen you for
> twenty-five years. Tell me, how is your son Harvey?"
> "Harvey? There's a son! He's a doctor with a terrific
> practice. Patients come to see him from all over the
> country." "Marvelous," responds the friend, "and what
> about Marvin?" "Marvin? He is a big lawyer. He takes
> cases right up to the Supreme Court." "My," says the
> friend admiringly, "and your son Herman?" "Herman is
> still Herman. Still a tailor," sighed the father, "and if it
> weren't for Herman, we'd all be starving."

One of the reasons that raising a child can be overwhelming
is that parents find it hard to keep their marital difficulties out
of the child rearing. They disagree about what is best for the
child, sometimes trying to use the youngster as an ally in a
war against the spouse. They can intensify each other's unresolved childhood conflicts as they argue about what is best for

the child. Sometimes they try to be tactful with each other but it often backfires.

> George comes home and is greeted by his wife Hilda who says, "Hi George, how was your day?" "The same as usual. How was it here at home?" "Well George, let's see, how can I break this to you? How many children do we have?" "What's this, a quiz?" the husband asks. "No George, I want to be tactful. How many children do we have, George?" "Four," replies George with irritation. "So sweetheart, three of them did not fall out of the tree and break a leg. Isn't that lovely?"

> One friend asks, "And how many children do you have?" "None," is the reply. "No children? So what do you do for aggravation?"

On many occasions parents and children do not see eye to eye on how the child should deal with school assignments.

> "Daddy, here's a note from the teacher," said Michael when he came home from school. "I'll read it to you, Daddy. 'Dear Mr. Lewis, Michael really ought to have the use of an encyclopedia.' Well, Daddy, what do you think?" Mr. Lewis, without lifting his head from the newpaper grunts, "I walked to school when I was a kid and so can you."

Sometimes the parent is an ally of the child as the latter copes with the vicissitudes of being a student.

> Abie brought home a note from his teacher that read, "Dear Mrs. Rosenblum, Your son Abraham has body odor. Please rectify the situation." Mrs. Rosenblum wrote back: "Dear Teacher, My Abie ain't no rose. Learn him, don't smell him."

A normal frustration for many parents is coping with the youngster's growing autonomy. Many parents experience the child's movement away from them as a severe narcissistic injury and react with strong separation anxiety. Leo Rosten (1968) tells the story of a Jewish mother who sent her "Bubeleh" (little doll) off to his first day of school with many hugs and a great deal of advice:

> "So, Bubeleh, you'll be a good boy and obey the teacher? And you won't make noise, Bubeleh, and be polite and play nice with the other children. And when it's time to come home, Bubeleh, you'll button up warm so you won't catch cold, Bubeleh, and you'll be careful crossing the street and come right home." When the boy returned from school that afternoon, his mother hugged and kissed him and then asked, "So did you like school, Bubeleh? You made new friends? You learned something?" "Yeah," said the little boy, "I learned my name is Irving."

Parents can continue to infantilize their offspring well into the child's adolescence and beyond.

> Some friends were visiting the Volgers and commented that they had never met the Volgers' son. They asked how old he is now. "Twenty-two," they were told. They wondered if they could meet him. The parents asked their servants to get Volger Jr. and a few minutes later he arrived being carried on a chair. The friends were embarrassed, and expressed their pity, "Oh too bad, doesn't he walk?" "Oh yes," said Mrs. Volger, "but thank God, he doesn't have to."

On the farm where children were economic assets, farmers had many kids. Yet urban parents try to use their offspring as economic assets too.

> When Mr. Percy's tax return was audited, the Internal Revenue Service questioned his deduction for his daughter

in 1988. The auditor reminded Mr. Percy that his daughter
was born in January, 1989. "So," Percy protested, "it was
last year's business."

Attitudes are changing but many parents still want their
children to marry within their own socioeconomic group, race,
and religion. When this does not take place many parents feel
humiliated and devastated. It is as if they have failed themselves.

> The phone rings. Mrs. Shulman answers and hears her
> daughter Sharon's voice. "Mama," she says, "I'm en-
> gaged." "*Mazel Tov*" [good luck], the mother enthusiasti-
> cally exclaims. "You have to realize something, Mama. My
> fiancé is not Jewish," Sharon hesitantly confides. Mrs.
> Shulman is quiet. Then Sharon says, "Also, he's unem-
> ployed and we don't have any money." "That's no prob-
> lem," says Mrs. Shulman. "You'll live in our house and can
> have our bedroom." "But where will you stay, Mama?"
> Mrs. Shulman explains, "Papa will sleep in the living
> room." "And what about you?" Sharon wants to know.
> "Oh don't worry about me," Mrs. Shulman states, "be-
> cause as soon as I get off the phone I'm going to kill
> myself."

Many parents indulge their children the way they wish they
had been indulged by their parents. They find it difficult to set
limits and seem frightened of getting their children angry at
them. A parent seeing a therapist in a child guidance clinic told
the interviewer, "My daughter has me wrapped around her
little finger. All I can do is just try to save face. When she
misbehaves I find myself saying to her, 'Would you mind
terribly going to your room at your convenience? Okay? Try to
be in your room, if you can, by the time your Dad counts to
1,500, okay?'"

For decades many people from many walks of life have
debated whether a divorce hinders a child's development more

or less than if two unhappy individuals stay married "just for the sake of the children." Some argue that children sense their parents' real feelings of hatred toward each other and being subjected to the parents' tensions every day is much worse than living through their parents' divorce. Others contend that children keep parents together and their presence can motivate the married couple to resolve some of their difficulties. There is no real answer to this issue because married couples and their children differ greatly and what is helpful to one family may be disastrous for another.

> A husband and wife appear before the judge because they want a divorce. After the judge ascertains that they are in their nineties, he asks how long they have been married. When he is told "Seventy-four years," he asks how long they have had marital conflict. They both say they have been unhappy for their entire marriage. "So why did you stay together so long?" the judge asks. The couple explains, "We decided to wait until the children were dead."

> One day when my mother-in-law was in her late eighties, she implied that she was insufficiently appreciated by her children. My brother-in-law, Elihu, said, "Mother, Marcia, Paul, and I sat down together and we agreed that you are an excellent mother." As my mother-in-law beamed, Elihu added, "The vote was two to one!"

Parents not only are concerned about how their children treat them while they are alive but they also have fantasies of how they will be respected after death. A friend told me his mother used to say, "I expect my children to pee on my grave."

> An elderly Jewish woman consults her rabbi and says to him, "I have two requests before I die. First, I want to be cremated." The rabbi tells her that cremation is forbidden in Jewish law. The lady insists and since the rabbi can't influence her he asks, "What is your second request?" "I

want my ashes scattered over Bloomingdale's." The rabbi wants to know, "Why would you do something like that?" "Because," the woman answers, "that way I'm sure my daughters will visit me at least twice a week."

Children's Frustrations

It is sometimes overlooked that part of being a mature individual is having the capacity to tolerate frustration. When we are born, we want what we want when we want it. Governed almost exclusively by the pleasure principle, it is never easy for us to accept the principles of reality. Yet, to grow old and develop, children need to accept being weaned from the breast or bottle, learn how to control themselves and adapt to toilet training, accept that they cannot have exclusive possession of their parents, become able to share with others, and a host of other necessary growing experiences that require taking on frustrations and deprivations.

Because coping with frustration and deprivation is an irritating fact of life, children can become very hateful and negativistic when they are confronted with it. They do not like taking "no" for an answer and are frequently trying to defy, upset, and demean parents and parental figures who they feel are the fomentors of their unhappiness.

Because rebelliousness of children emanating from their conflicts is a universal fact of life causing conflict to adults, there are many jokes that have childhood rebellion as their major theme.

Two boys about 12 years old were talking about how difficult home and school were, how no one understood them at either place, and how much they wanted to chuck it all and run away. Finally one of the boys blurted out, "Let's do it. Let's run away!" "Run away?" asked the second boy, "our fathers will find us and beat the hell out of us." "So," replied the first youngster, "we'll hit them back." "What? Hit your father? You must be crazy!" retorted the friend. "Have you forgotten one of the most important of the Ten Commandments—always honor your father and mother?" The initiator of the plot thought silently for a moment and then suggested, "So you hit my father and I'll hit yours."

Very often resentment that cannot be discharged at home is expressed in the classroom.

A third-grade teacher asked her class, "Who said 'Give me liberty or give me death'?" For several moments silence reigned until it was broken by a Japanese boy who said, "Patrick Henry, 1776." "Wonderful!" said the teacher. Then she admonished the entire class, "You should all be ashamed of yourselves. Here you are, all Americans, and not one of you knows the answer. It took a boy of Japanese descent to give the right answer." As the teacher turned to write something on the blackboard, a youngster called out, "Fuck the Japs!" The teacher irately turned and asked, "Who said that?" The culprit retorted, "General Douglas MacArthur, 1942."

What is going on in the home can be surmised by children's productions in the classroom.

A new teacher was eager to enrich the curriculum and decided to bring in hands-on experiences for her first grade class. She brought in three kinds of meat and passed out small samples to every child. When she asked if they recognized the first sample, many hands went up to show they knew it was pork. The second sample, roast beef, got fewer hands but still a good response. On the third sample, venison, the children chewed vigorously, but no one recognized deer meat. Finally the teacher said, "I will give you a hint. What does your mother call your father?"

One youngster jumped up shouting, "Spit it out! Spit it out! It's asshole!"

Parents and teachers learn, as do therapists and others who want to help people modify attitudes and behavior, that long lectures rarely influence children or adults to mend their ways. Often admonishing somebody can exacerbate the problem.

> A father was berating his son for always putting things off. "I don't know what's going to become of you. You procrastinate all the time." Responded the son, "Just you wait and see."

Mastering toilet training is difficult for children. They would rather urinate and defecate wherever and whenever the urge hits them.

> The teacher was telling her first-grade class the appropriate way to get her attention if they had to go to the bathroom. She explained slowly and clearly, "Class, if you have to make a sissy, please raise one finger, and if you have to make a doody, you raise two fingers. I hope everybody understands this." The children seemed to grasp the concepts and were using their fingers appropriately. After a few days a youngster was frantically waving both his hands. The teacher empathetically asked, "Brucie, what seems to be on your mind?" "Quick, give me a number! I got to fart."

Next to adults, children feel vulnerable and powerless. Because of the tremendous discrepancy between them, children often try to embarrass adults and make them feel weak. Here is George Jessel's favorite story:

> Ronald, a little boy about 4 years old, often spoke impulsively and was reprimanded several times a day by adults. Ronald was visiting his aunt and uncle who had guests for

lunch. Ronald turned to his aunt and said, "Auntie, I want to tinkle." She took him aside and said, "Never say that. If you want to tinkle say, 'I want to whisper.'" That night when Aunt and Uncle were sleeping, Ronald got into bed with them, pulled on his Uncle's shoulder and said, "Uncle, I want to whisper." The uncle said, "All right, Ronny, don't wake your aunt. Whisper in my ear." Ronald was returned to his parents the next day.

A favorite story of mine is one I heard when I was 8 years old:

Alvin, a 9-year-old boy, was very careless with his language. Although his parents tried very hard to curb his obscenity, they were unsuccessful. Finally the mother tried something new, "a game of substitutes." One day when Alvin said "shit," Mother said, "Every time you want to say 'shit,' say 'meat' instead, okay?" Alvin liked the idea and every time he was frustrated he would say, "Aw, meat!" The program was working and Alvin's mother worked to increase his repertoire of substitutes. When Alvin said "bastard," Mother taught him to say "priest" instead. When he said "fuck" he was told to say "wash." After the system was working very well, Alvin's parents had their clergyman to dinner. Alvin greeted the clergyman, "Hello you bastard. We are having shit for dinner. My mother is fucking Johnny."

One of Sigmund Freud's favorite jokes involving childish rebellion is this one:

Itzig is asked in school, "Who was Moses?" "Moses was the son of an Egyptian princess." "That's not true," replies the teacher. "Moses was the son of a Hebrew mother. The Egyptian princess found the baby in a basket." But Itzig responds, "Says she."

Woody Allen (1971, 1975, 1980) in his books and movies is forever dealing with childish rebellion frequently making himself the angry child. In one of his monologues, Woody pulls out an expensive watch and says, "You should see this while I've got it out. . . . This speaks for breeding and it's mine. . . . Actually my grandfather sold me this watch on his deathbed."

On another occasion Woody told his audience about being kidnapped. It went something like this. "And they drive me off and send a ransom note to my parents. My father has bad reading habits. So he got into bed that night with the ransom note and read about half of it, then got drowsy and fell asleep. Meanwhile they take me to New Jersey bound and gagged. My parents finally realize that I'm kidnapped and they snap into action. They rent out my room."

Of all the stories I am familiar with in which a child tries to humiliate an adult, I know of none other where the adult gets his comeuppance so unmercifully. This is from Maude Thickett's (1983) *Outrageously Offensive Jokes*:

> A man spending the afternoon with his married lover hears her husband return unexpectedly. He hops out of bed, grabs his clothes, and ducks into the closet. Behind him he hears a whisper, "Boy, it sure is dark in here." "Who's that?" "My name is Johnny and I live here. Do you wanna buy my marble collection? Only a hundred bucks." "A hundred bucks? Are you crazy?" asks the man. "Well, if you're not interested, maybe my father . . . " "No, wait. Here's the hundred bucks. Now shut up." Two days later in the same bed, the man hears his lover's husband return. Again he takes cover in the closet, and hears a small voice behind him say, "Boy, it sure is dark in here." "You again?" "Yeah, and this time I'm selling my baseball card collection." "How much this time?" "Two hundred, inflation you know." "Jesus, here. Now shut up." The next day the boy boasts about his windfall to his father who says, "I don't know what you did to get that much money but it couldn't have been honest. You better go to confession."

> When the boy takes his place in the confessional box he
> says in a whisper, "Boy, it sure is dark in here." At that the
> priest's partition opens with a bang and the priest says,
> "Are you going to start that shit again?" [p. 84]

Accompanying rebellious wishes toward parents usually
comes guilt and self-hatred. Telushkin (1992) quotes the car-
toonist Jules Feiffer who put these words into the mouth of one
of his characters: "I grew up to have my father's looks, my
father's speech patterns, my father's posture, my father's
opinion, and my mother's contempt for my father."

Children's Conceptions and Misconceptions

In the process of growing up, children do not learn perfectly.
They have many different notions about nature, nurture,
concepts, words, and interpersonal relationships, all of which
are not purely objective. Their maturational patterns vary a
great deal so that two children of the same age may have very
different levels of comprehension about many issues.

> When two 8-year-olds were conversing, one said, "I found
> a condom on the patio last night." "Oh," said his friend,
> "what's a patio?"

When we think of children's conceptions and misconceptions we are reminded of course of the many different ways
that children describe sex and the birth process. I remember
seeing a cartoon in the *New Yorker* magazine a few years ago in
which one boy says to the other, "You know my mother is a
virgin." And I enjoyed the remark of a little girl in therapy
many years ago. When I asked her if she knew the difference

between boys and girls she responded, "Oh course, dummy! Boys don't have vaginas."

In this day and age children do not just talk about sex and marriage. They actively consider it.

> A 5-year-old boy asked his father for $10. "What is it for, son?" asked his father. "It's so Stephanie and I can get married. She's going to ask her father for $10 too." "Well," said the father, "that's not a lot of money. What if you have a baby?" The 5-year-old answered, "Well, we've been lucky so far."

> A young boy lived alone with his mother. For several nights in a row he heard his mother desperately crying out, "I need a man! I need a man!" The cries ceased one night and the boy became curious. He posted himself by his mother's bedroom, and sure enough, he heard his mother conversing with a man. He looked through the keyhole and saw his mother making love with the man. The next night there were cries coming from the boy's room: "I need a bicycle! I need a bicycle!"

Sometimes what children want to know is not well understood by their parents.

> Little Joey asked his father "What does fornication mean?" The father was embarrassed and started to talk about the birds and bees, love, procreation, and numerous other dimensions of the reproductive process. Seeing that Joey was growing impatient, Father finally asked Joey, "Why do you want to know?" "I was at assembly today in school and we were celebrating Columbus Day. The principal said, 'For an occasion like this we should all be proud.'"

When I was 12 years old, a friend told me about the little boy who wanted a watch for Christmas, so his parents let him.

Little Susie asked her mother, "When I went into your room I saw Daddy's penis in your vagina. What do you do that for?" Mother answered, "That's the way you get a baby." A few days later, Susie asked, "Mother, yesterday I saw Daddy's penis in your mouth. What do you do that for?" Mother answered, "That's the way you get jewelry."

I remember the following riddle from my childhood.

Question: Why did the little boy think his father had two penises? Answer: He saw him use a small one to pee with, and a big one for brushing the babysitter's teeth.

One of the most obvious characteristics of growing children is that they frequently misunderstand the meaning of words and have difficulty pronouncing them. The child psychologist Arthur Jersild (1949) in his book *Child Psychology*, gives several examples in his text.

In reciting the pledge of allegiance to the flag, a child said, "I pledge a legion to the flag and to the Republic of Richard Sands, one nation and a vegetable with liberty and justice for all."

Another youngster substituted for "long to reign over us" from the British national anthem "long train run over us." In a genuinely patriotic manner, a little girl sang, "I love thy rots and chills" instead of "rocks and rills" from "America the Beautiful." Reciting "The Night Before Christmas" a little boy recited, "I rushed to the window and vomited (threw up) in the sash." Singing "The Star Spangled Banner," a lad chanted, "The grandpas we watched were so gallantly screaming."

In not quite deciphering the proper meaning of certain words, one child defined a pioneer as one "who moves father (farther) west." A 2-year-old boy at the dinner table folded his hands and assumed a devotional attitude when his mother asked whether he would like some pears (prayers). A school child told his teacher that the abbreviation for Illinois was "sick" (ill). In singing a solemn hymn, Clarence blurted out something about "a cross-eyed bear" (cross I'd bear). Referring to Jesus' twelve "bicycles" (disciples), a youngster talked about "a wonderful guy (guide) is he."

Getting in touch with a child's mode of reasoning is not always easy for adults.

> A nun asked a youngster, "Do you say a prayer before you eat?" The child replied, "No, my mother's a very good cook."

> A teacher asked the class, "What happened in the year 1809?" John answered, "Lincoln was born." The teacher smiled and said, "Good, John, now can you tell us what happened in 1812?" John, counting on his fingers, replied, "Lincoln had his third birthday."

> Another teacher asks her class, "What do you think Julius Caesar would be doing if he were alive today?" Mike answers, "He'd be drawing his old-age pension."

Another interesting characteristic of children is that they can overidentify with adults they idealize. A child playing Superman or Batman in many ways believes he is the character he's portraying. I remember when my sons were in their latency period (between 6 and 10 years old), if they were enacting the roles of Batman and Robin and we wanted them to come to dinner, calling them by their own names would be to no avail. We got a prompt response by calling "Batman and Robin."

> A 12-year-old had to give a speech at school on Abraham Lincoln. Unfortunately he left all of his notes at home. He started his speech with much hesitation saying in a stammer, "Abraham Lincoln died in 1865." Then he repeated,

"Abraham Lincoln died in 1865." He couldn't think of what else to say except, "And you know, I don't feel so good myself."

A teacher was berating Jimmy for his mispronunciation of words and poor diction. "Don't you know the King's English?" she asked him with a sneer. "Sure," replied Jimmy, "and so is the Queen."

Leo Rosten (1985) reproduces many letters from youngsters who are at camp and are writing to their parents. A postcard from a 10-year-old at camp for the first time reads, "Dear Folks, Having okay time, I think. Yesterday we went on a hike. Send my other sneaker. Love, Ricky." A letter from an 11-year-old reads: "Dear Ma, Remember what I told you if you made me go to camp? Something terrible would happen, I told you! Okay. It did. Love, Peter." And a postcard after three long weeks of silence from a 9-year-old at camp for the first time: "Dear Mother and Daddy, The Direcktor is making everyone write home. Eve" (pp. 84–85).

Children love to tell their own jokes, which usually take the form of riddles.

Question: What did the rug say to the floor? Answer: Stick 'em up, I got you covered. Question: Why did the ram fall over the cliff? Answer: He didn't see the ewe turn. Question: Mr. and Mrs. Bigger had a baby. Now who is the biggest in the family? Answer: The baby daughter because she was a little Bigger.

The following jokes all come back to me as ones I heard when I was in the fifth grade.

There was a girl by the name of Mary Dam. Each night before she went to sleep she would say her prayers: "God bless Mother Dam, God bless Father Dam, and God bless sister Dam." One night she was so tired she said, "God bless the whole Dam family."

A boy said to his father, "Dad, I want a quarter for being good." Replied the father, "When I was a boy, I was good for nothing."

A father sent his son to college and spent thousands of dollars. All he got was a quarterback.

One painter to another who is standing on top of a stepladder painting the ceiling: "Hold onto your brush, George, I'm going to borrow your ladder."

Question one: What would you do if you saw a bear? Answer: Run. Question two: What, with a bear behind?

The Child in the Adult

All clinicians are keenly aware of the fact that the child in the adult remains very much alive. Even when adults are in their forties, fifties, or sixties, they relate to their parents in a way that is quite similar to how they interacted with them when they were 4, 5, and 6. As we examine our patients' transference reactions we note the many ways that mature adults want to be fed, stroked, caressed, and be a favorite infant. And as we observe our own countertransference reactions, we note similar childish responses in ourselves.

In a *New York Times* article, "Toy Makers Meet the Inner Child," Calvin Sims (1992) wrote:

Many children are confronting a new frustration. Their parents are buying toys—for themselves. More and more adults are joining a trend that toy makers and students of pop culture say reflects the aging of baby boomers—a generation loath to grow old and searching for new ways to escape the stresses of the workplace.

It was Dorothy Parker who once said, "The only difference between men and boys is the cost and number of their
toys!" Were she alive today, Miss Parker might want to
broaden that, considering the rising number of men and
women buying toy cars, Barbie dolls, stuffed animals, and
electronic video games for themselves.

This month's issue of American Demographics magazine
reports that nearly half, 45 percent, of 20,000 adults sur-
veyed nationwide said they had bought a toy or game for
themselves or an adult friend in a typical year. [Ideas and
Trends, December 27, p. 12]

It has been clear to psychotherapists and others that the
assumption that children play and adults do not is definitely
false. There are many jokes that recognize how much of the
child remains in the adult and is very active. Here is one joke
that I have heard and told many times:

A mother goes into her son's room saying, "You have to
get up and go to school, Norman." Norman pulls his
blanket over his head and says, "I don't want to go to
school." "You have to go to school," the mother insists,
"you're the principal."

As clinicians know, problems around dirt and cleanliness
abound in adults because they are still in many ways children
who do not know whether "to shit all over the place" or obey
the strict voices of their superego.

Two men go into a restaurant and the first asks for tea. The
second also asks for tea. "And make sure the glass is
clean," he tells the waiter. When the waiter returns with
two glasses of tea he asks, "Which one of you wanted the
clean glass?"

Another of Freud's favorite jokes deals with the strong
infantile dependency wishes in adults.

> A *shnorrer* (beggar) is accustomed to receiving a set dona-
> tion from a man every week of the year. One day when he
> comes for the money, the man tells him that he can't give
> him anything. "I've had terrible expenses recently. My
> wife became very sick and I had to send her to a health
> resort in Carlsbad. It's very cold there so I had to buy her
> new clothes and a fur coat." "What!" yelled the beggar,
> "with my money?!"

Many times adults will complain about their mothers or
fathers and sound as if they were children having a temper
tantrum. A patient of mine whom I'll call Arnold Blume, about
40 years old, was yelling and screaming about his mother.
"There's not a lot of warmth between me and my mother. I
wanted to discuss it with her. I said, 'Mrs. Blume . . . '"

Although adults tend to deny the existence of the child in
themselves, they nonetheless try to look as young as possible,
revealing their secret wish to be a child again.

> Mr. Sternberg, a man in his seventies, was sitting near the
> pool of a resort hotel. He could not help noticing the white-
> haired man at the next table who sat with two beautiful
> women every day during the week, drinking, and laughing,
> and eating. The same white-haired man went off the big
> diving board every day and swam several laps without
> stopping. Every night he was dancing until the wee hours
> in the nightclub. After noticing this man going through this
> arduous schedule for two weeks, Sternberg went over to
> him and said admiringly, "Mister, it's amazing the condi-
> tion you are in!" "Thank you," said the white-haired man.
> "Excuse me for asking but how old are you?" queried Stern-
> berg. The man shrugged, "Twenty eight."

Parents identify with their sons and daughters until death!
This is one of the reasons why some parents tend to be quite
critical of their sons- or daughters-in-law. They want their
offspring to be indulged the way they wanted to be indulged in
their own marriages.

Mrs. Plotnick meets Mrs. Silver. "Tell me," says Mrs. Plotnick, "what happened to your son?" "My son, what a misfortune," laments Mrs. Silver. "He married a girl who doesn't lift a finger around the house. She can't cook, can't sew, all she does is nap. My poor son brings her breadfast in bed, and all day long she stays in there, loafing, reading, eating bon-bons." "How awful," says Mrs. Plotnick. "And how is your daughter?" "Ah, my daughter!" smiles Mrs. Silver. "She married a perfect man, a saint. He won't let her go into the kitchen, he gives her a maid, a cook, and a nurse for the children. Every morning he brings her breakfast in bed! And he makes her stay in bed all day, relaxing, reading."

Depending on parents to gratify childish wishes when one is a mature adult can at times be risky.

Mrs. Solomon dialed her daughter and said, "Hello, darling. This is your mama. How's by you?" The daughter responded, "Mama, everything is just terrible. The children are acting up, the house is messy, I have a bad cold, and I have women coming over today for a Sisterhood luncheon." "Don't worry, darling," said the mother. "I'll take two subways and two busses and walk the mile to your house. I'll take care of the children, clean up your house, make you chicken soup for your cold, and make a nice lunch for the Sisterhood." "Oh, Mama, you are a real dear." "It's all right, darling, I'll be glad to do it. And by the way, how's Sam?" "Sam?" the daughter asks. "Who's Sam?" "Your husband, Sam," snaps the mother. "But my husband's name is Lou," replies the young woman anxiously. "Is this Beverly seven, seven six seven six?" asks the mother. "No," the girl answers. "Oh my God, I got the wrong number," says the mother. "Wait, please," wails the young woman. "Does that mean you aren't coming?"

Finding the Child in Ourselves

Many years ago I heard a talk by the well-known psychologist Gordon Allport, who reported on his one consultation with

Freud. At the consultation, Allport spent a long time describing a young boy he had just seen on the bus while traveling to Freud's office. After Allport spoke in detail about the boy, Freud asked, "Are you that boy?"

Soon after I heard that story I realized that the jokes we tell about children tell us something about the child in ourselves. I recall when my son began coaching young boys he told me this joke.

> Seven-year-old Rolphie was a belligerent boy who constantly cursed. It was difficult for his parents and teachers to limit him. He went on cursing. One day the teacher was trying to help the class master the alphabet. She asked the class to give her a word that begins with "A." When Rolphie raised his hand, the teacher thought of the curse words starting with "A" that he might use, and called on Mabel instead. "Apple" was the word given. Then the teacher asked for a word starting with "B." When Rolphie raised his hand, the teacher thought of the words that Rolphie might say, and called on David, who said, "Baseball." The lesson continued this way and the teacher kept ignoring Rolphie's hand waving to give the answer. By the time she got to "R," every other student had had a turn, so she took a deep breath and called on Rolphie. "Rats," he said to her relief. As she praised him for his answer, he went on to say, "Yeah, rats, they're big motherfuckers with long dicks."

What does this joke tell about the child in my son and in me? Obviously it caters to our joint wishes to rebel against authority. Although there is some desire to conform, the wish to defy in a phallic exhibitionistic manner wins. Being ignored is not pleasant and the Rolphie in us lets the world know this.

Giving the child in us some pleasure helps reduce the strain in being an adult.

5

Thank God I'm an Atheist: Religious and Racial Issues

Despite the fact that in our essentially liberal, ethical, and egalitarian society religion is sometimes dismissed, the influence of traditional religious ideas quietly, often invisibly, permeates many areas of our lives. The majority of Americans have been brought up in one or another of the traditional religions, and the values they have learned in their churches or synagogues as well as the customs, rituals, and ceremonies still profoundly affect their attitudes and behavior. Americans are among the most religiously aware citizens in the Western world, with more than half of the total population belonging to a church or synagogue. In the 1980s the total church or synagogue membership was estimated to be over 130,000,000 people; in a typical week about 40 percent of adults in America attended a church or synagogue (Kaye 1980). It is still quite important for an American presidential candidate, or anybody who aspires to be a political official, to demonstrate some form of religious affiliation. To be acceptable to the masses, it is necessary to accept some form of religion.

In a series of papers Freud (1909, 1919, 1937b) provided us with much understanding of why religion retains much psychological value to the human race, comprised of specimens who are very vulnerable and imperfect. The search for consolation in the face of threatening feelings of inadequacy and helplessness, for which religion provides an answer, is nothing new in life since people find themselves in a similar situation of helplessness as children vis-à-vis parents. When young children recognize they are not omnipotent and are unable to get everything they want, they unconsciously give up their own sense of omnipotence and believe their parents are superhuman. The wish for a powerful parent who will love us, protect us, gratify our wishes, and give us strength is not relinquished very easily.

The dynamically oriented clinician views the longing for a strong parent as closely related to the longing for a father who is King of the Universe. The wisdom and goodness that are attributed to the deity reduce our anxiety concerning the dangers of life much like the child feels protected by the wisdom and goodness of an omnipotent and omniscient parent. When life is difficult and painful, when we cannot fend for ourselves, God, our omnipotent parental figure, can be a form of valuable sustenance.

Religious adherence emanates from more than a wish to depend on a strong parent. Religion is also regarded as a societal institution that propounds ethical and moral values and denounces others. Many of the ethical and moral commitments that are part of our superego are often considered religious values. That is why many individuals who are not adherents of any organized religious group will refer to themselves nonetheless as religious. When we adhere to the voices of our superego, all of us, regardless of our formal religious affiliations, feel better. Religious individuals hope that Providence is watching over them and will reward them in a future existence. As Freud (1937b) pointed out, the ordinary person cannot imagine life without this Providence. He is a greatly exalted Father who tends to His children and is softened by their prayers and placated by the signs of their guilt.

Yet the notion of a God stirs up conflict for almost every mortal. If God is an omnipotent and omniscient being, then theists can be furious with Him for all the evil in the world and all the wishes He has not granted. However, atheists and agnostics often envy those who appear to be comforted by this powerful parent while they, the infidels, feel orphaned and abandoned. The ambivalence that the theist and atheist often feel about their respective positions has led to bitter disputes and even wars. Because a belief or disbelief in God, from a psychodynamic view, cannot be easily carried out without conflict, the figure of God is the butt of many jokes. Many of us feel ambivalent toward Him. He is exalted but disappoints; He is everywhere but nowhere.

When individuals are full of doubt about their loyalties and ambivalent about their fates, to strengthen themselves they can become competitive, arrogant, and demeaning of others. This is seen among religious groups and even within the same sect. No one needs much convincing to note the warring factions among the millions who adhere to the notions of "Love thine enemies," and "Turn the other cheek." Those who are familiar with the history and sociology of Judaism are aware of the intense competition between Orthodox, Conservative, and Reform Jews.

One of the major reasons why religion sparks many conflicts is that people are not free to question the platitudes of their own faiths. Jews are "God's chosen people" and there is no debating it as far as authorities on Judaic law are concerned. "Black is beautiful," and African-Americans try their best to convice themselves and everyone else of this. Allah knows it all, Shinto contains the truth, and Jesus is for sure the son of God.

In "Moses and Monotheism," Freud (1937b) described "The People of Israel" and said the following about the Jews:

> There is no doubt that they have a particularly high opinion of themselves, that they regard themselves as more distinguished, of higher standing, as superior to other people—from whom they are also distinguished by

many of their customs. At the same time they are inspired
by a peculiar confidence in life, such as is derived from the
secret ownership of some precious possession. . . . We
may assert it was the man Moses who imprinted this trait
upon the Jewish people. He raised their self-esteem by
assuring them that they were God's chosen people. [pp.
105–106]

When religious or racial groups believe they are chosen, are
more beautiful, or have a monopoly on the truth, they provoke
dissent and animosity in others. Living in the twentieth century society that champions egalitarianism makes it increas-
ingly difficult for most of us to endorse the idea that any person
or any group is superior to another. The notion of superiority
is often equated with Nazism and Hitler and most of us abhor
the association. A half century ago the social scientist Myrdal
(1944) noted in *An American Dilemma* that equalitarianism is part
of the American creed. In American society the equality theme
stresses the similar intrinsic value of every man and woman
and is combined with a resentment of any claim to social
distinction or special status not earned or based upon particular
merit, a factor that the social psychologist Gorer (1948) argues
militates against religious groups like the Jews.

To ambivalence about God and ethnocentrism, we may add
another variable in religious matters that sparks both interpersonal and intrapsychic conflict, namely, scientific rationalism
(Sklare 1960). This influence has been especially strong in
American society where the virtues of modern science are daily
extolled in the schools and the mass media. Many individuals
living in the twentieth century find it difficult to reconcile the
teachings of biology, physics, and psychoanalysis with biblical
and other religious teachings. Skepticism that results from
exposure to scientific rationalism is of course not limited to a
questioning of the Bible's accuracy; it tends to be diffused
throughout other religious beliefs and practices as well.

The more we examine religion psychologically and sociologically, the more we appreciate how very conflicted most of us are on the subject. Two popular novels by Herman Wouk, *The Caine Mutiny* and *Marjorie Morningstar*, demonstrate through their main characters how many of us are concomitantly rebelling and conforming when it comes to religious and moral values. In both of these novels, as the leading characters' guilt mounts they beat themselves for their rebellious actions and eventually submit compliantly to their parental figures' dictates. Their struggles are our struggles and are perhaps close to universal. It should be noted that this is also the story of Herman Wouk himself. An Orthodox Jew, Wouk married a Gentile woman. After a short period of marriage he insisted that his wife convert and fervently practice all of the Orthodox Jewish rituals.

This cursory review of religion should help us better appreciate the fact that the institution arouses many conflicts for most of us. Although religion attempts to help people deal with the pains and aches of standing alone and provides support in times of need (Nass 1949), the kind of support it offers is not always palliative to many. Despite the fact that religions provide individuals with the opportunity to share with others and belong to a group (Fromm 1950), group affiliations also activate resentment in outsiders and help create enemies. Though religion attempts to give answers to questions about the mysteries of life, its precepts often collide with those of scientific rationalism.

The many jokes that deal with religious and racial matters tend to focus on the conflicts and problems we have just discussed. Let us first consider some of the jokes that deal with God.

Who Is God and Where Is He?

In the 1960s there was a much discussed newspaper article pointing out that God is still alive and resides in Argentina! The reason this article induced everything from laughter to resentment, serious discussion to superficial banter, belief to disbelief, may be explained, in part, by the many doubts that the faithful and the unfaithful have about God and His powers. Most jokes about God attempt to question His supreme strength and try to make Him appear human and with foibles.

> Father O'Brien, a well-known priest, went to his eternal resting place to meet his Maker. Although pronounced dead, communication between God and some prominent Roman Catholic officials brought the world-shaking news that Father O'Brien was going to be brought back to life. At the appointed time a number of priests and nuns gathered around to observe Father O'Brien's return to earth. As he arose from his deep slumber and slowly opened his eyes, his eager colleagues had one question. Represented by a renowned bishop, the question was, "What is God like?" Father O'Brien heaved a deep sigh and said hesitantly, "Well, She's black."

The joke clearly mocks the Caucasian, patrocentric view that God is white and male. It humanizes Him by giving Him the characteristics that many white males might fear, and humanizing Him in this way is the theme of many jokes.

> A pious nun died and went to heaven. At the gate Saint Peter greeted her with much enthusiasm since she had been a kind, virtuous, and devoted person on earth. "The Lord has directed that you may have any wish granted here in heaven," Peter told her. The nun replied, "All my life I have wished to meet Mary, the Mother of our Savior." Within moments her wish was granted and she was able to ask Mary any question she wished. "Mary, Mother of our Lord, what was it like giving birth to our Savior, Jesus Christ?" Mary was quiet for a moment and then said, "To tell you the truth, I was hoping for a girl."

What transpires in heaven is probably a fantasy of all children and many adults. The situation is often used to poke fun at a particular group.

> When President Ulysses Grant, a former general in the army, went to heaven, he was immediately informed that in contrast to his life on earth where he received special treatment, in heaven all are equal. He was directed to get on the end of the line that was leading into the cafeteria. Chafing at the bit at the lack of special consideration, Grant observed a man in a white gown with a stethoscope on his chest cutting into line ahead of everyone else. Grant protested and a man standing next to him explained what was happening. "The man in the white coat with the stethoscope? That's God, he thinks he's a doctor!"

Just as heaven and its environs have been a dominant fantasy of many, so has hell. Hell on earth has been the subject of many jokes.

> When a henpecked husband died and went to hell, he immediately started giving orders and bossing everyone around. "Stop it," said Satan, "one would think you owned the place." "I do," said the man, "my wife gave it to me while I was on earth."

Red Skelton once asked, "People in hell—where do they tell people to go?" When I was a child talking to my friend about whether I would go to heaven or hell, my friend said, "I'm scared that I'll meet God and He'll sneeze and I won't know what to say."

Not only have there been many attempts to humanize God, but similar attempts have been made with other religious figures such as Jesus and Moses.

> Jesus and Moses decided to play a round of golf. When they approached the first tee, Jesus took out his three iron

and hit the ball straight down the fairway. Before the ball landed a squirrel caught it, dashed up a tree with the golf ball, hurled it to a rabbit who ran it to the green and dropped it in the hole for a hole in one. Moses turned to Jesus and inquired, "Are you going to play golf, or are you going to fuck around?"

In attempts to make Jesus one of their own, both Jews and Christians have made many claims on him. Christians are certain that he is the son of God but Jews are equally certain that he was a model Jewish man.

Jewish people ask, "How do you know Jesus was Jewish?" The proof is that he was in his thirties, unmarried, still living with his mother. He went into his father's business, thought his mother was a virgin, and his mother thought he was God.

Jews and Christians have debated who is the Messiah and when is he coming to visit earth. Because prophesies about the Messiah were not fulfilled during Jesus's time, Jews have laid claim to him. Rabbi Telushkin (1992) tells the folowing story of the Messiah:

In a small Russian community, the council decides to pay a poor Jew a ruble a week to sit at the town's entrance and be the first to greet the Messiah when he arrives. The man's brother comes to see him and is puzzled why he took such a low-paying job. "It's true," the poor man responds, "the pay is low. But it's a steady job."

One of the reasons many people sustain their belief in God is because they are confident He will answer their prayers. Many individuals ascribe to God the quality of a benign parent who will reward the pure in heart and punish the evil.

> A man was pleading with God, "How come, God, I am such a good man who works hard, generous to my family, prays to you four times a day from work as well as twice a day in the temple, and you give me nothing? While my brother who is a crook, a lowlife, is selfish and mean, you give all the worldly possessions? Why, God? Why, God?" the man beseeched. A few moments later after some rumbling in the sky, a voice resounds, "Because you *noodge* me too much."

Many people visualize themselves as servants of God. The more servile they are and the more masochistically they behave, the more they believe they will have an opportunity to receive God's blessing.

> During a service on Yom Kippur [the Day of Atonement], the holiest day in the Jewish year, the rabbi of the congregation went into a chant, beating his breast and praying, "Oh, God, forgive me. I am a nothing, a nothing who is unworthy of your loving kindness." Then the cantor followed and prayed, "Oh my rock and my redeemer, I pray that you hear me. I am a nothing, a nothing." Following this the president of the congregation bellowed, "Oh, supreme King of Kings, Lord of the universe, I am a nothing, a nothing." When the president of the congregation concluded his lamentations, a very poor and disheveled man went in front of the congregation and prayed, "Oh Lord, forgive me, I am a nothing, a nothing." With that the president turned to the rabbi and protested, "Look who has the *chutzpah* [nerve] to call himself a nothing!"

The Clergy

Rabbis, ministers, priests, and other members of the clergy are considered to be God's representatives on earth. As such, they

are endowed with some of the same attributes of God—
omnipotence, omniscience, reverence, brilliance, powers to
forgive, and many other grandiose qualities. As a consequence,
similar to God, they are demeaned for their imperfections,
taunted for their humanness, and criticized when their wisdom
demonstrates some flaws. As representatives of God on earth,
they are often the recipients of confessions.

> MacDonald and McQueen went to see the priest to make
> their confessions. MacDonald went first and revealed to
> the priest that he had committed adultery, but he could not
> reveal the name of the woman involved. The priest asked,
> "Was it Mrs. O'Shaughnessy?" MacDonald replied, "No,
> Father." The priest tried again, "Was it Mrs. Flaherty?"
> Again MacDonald answered, "No, Father." The priest
> implored his congregant to try to expose the name of the
> woman and told him he would be forgiven if he told
> the name and recited three Hail Marys. He couldn't and
> the priest tried one last time, "Was it Mrs. Donovan?" "No,
> Father," again from MacDonald. The priest could not
> forgive him. When MacDonald met McQueen outside the
> confession booth he was asked, "Were you forgiven?"
> "No," he answered, "but I got three new good names."

Just as when children feel ambivalence confessing misdeeds
to their parents, parishioners experience something similar
when confessing to a clergyman. It is like facing one's superego. The guilt activates a fear of punishment so one often
withholds information. Yet there is a wish to confess so that
one will have a clearer conscience. Leo Rosten (1985) tells the
following story:

> Mickey Mitganger went to a rabbi to confess his sins but he
> was so ashamed that he said, "Rabbi I didn't come here for
> myself but for a friend. He asked me to come. He told me
> everything to ask you." The rabbi thought over this strange
> request and asked, "What sins has your friend commit-

ted?" "He often takes the name of the Lord in vain. He fornicates— and gambles—and he even—" "Stop," sighed the rabbi, "your friend is foolish. Why didn't he come here himself?" "He's too ashamed . . . " "But," said the rabbi with a smile, "he could have told me that he came for you thus saving you all this embarrassment."

One of the clergyman's major functions is to deliver inspiring sermons that are designed to strengthen the congregation's devotion to and involvement in the church or synagogue. It also helps the clergyman gain status among the congregants, thereby securing for him tenure and future economic security.

Reverend Smith was about to be fired unless he could deliver more stimulating sermons. He decided to discuss his problem with a mentor, his former teacher, who suggested that one of the things that makes a sermon go better is if an alcoholic drink is taken about 20 minutes before giving the sermon. Although he never imbibed, Reverend Smith felt desperate enough to go along with his mentor's prescription. The mentor also agreed to sit in on the sermon in case he could come up with additional suggestions to improve the sermons. After Reverend Smith gave a very stimulating sermon, the mentor reviewed it with him. "All in all, it was a spirited sermon. The only correction I would make is that 'David slew Goliath.' He didn't 'pound the shit' out of him."

The president of the congregation was speaking to their Japanese rabbi. "It is with much regret that I have to inform you that we must dismiss you." "Oh," said the rabbi, "you don't like Bar Mitzvahs?" The president assured the rabbi that he did a good job at Bar Mitzvahs. "Oh," said the Rabbi, "you don't like funerals?" Again the president assured the rabbi his officiating at funerals was competent. The devout Japanese rabbi was even more mystified since the president told him he did well at weddings and sermons. The president finally explained, "You see, Rabbi,

it's the way you do circumcisions. You raise your hand like
a karate chop and shout 'A . . . cha!'"

One of the many ways that the laity demonstrate their
hostility to the clergy is by making them sexual beings. In most
religions the clergy are supposed to be very careful about
monitoring their sexual impulses and in some sects they vow to
be celibate. To make a priest, nun, rabbi, or minister a normal
sexual being is to demote and demean him or her.

A minister, priest, and rabbi were going by train from New
York City to Pittsburgh to an interdenominational conference. When they met at the information booth at Grand
Central Station, the minister decided he would buy the
tickets for all three of them. At the ticket booth he saw a
scantily clad, sexy young woman selling the tickets, and he
requested, "Three tickets to Titsburgh, please." Embarrassed, he left the booth and confided to his colleagues
what had transpired. The rabbi went over to get the
tickets, and saw, indeed, what a buxom lass the clerk was.
In a very dignified voice he asked for "three tickets to
Pittsburgh," and was quite pleased with himself. He put
down a fifty dollar bill and said, "Could you give me the
change please in nipples and dimes?" Ashamed of his slip,
he returned to his colleagues without the tickets, and it
remained for the priest to purchase their tickets. He
admonished the young woman, "You should be ashamed
of yourself dressing this way! It is sacrilegious. Do you
realize St. Finger is pointing his peter at you?"

Three clergymen decided to make a secret visit to a
whorehouse. When the priest exited, his two colleagues
wondered how much it cost him. "Twenty-four dollars,"
he told them. The other clergymen wanted to know how
that amount was determined. "You get charged two dollars per inch," he explained. The minister had his turn and
reported he was charged twenty dollars. When the rabbi
left and reported his cost, the others were astonished that

it was only six dollars. He explained, "You fellows paid both ways but I only paid on the way out."

Usually when a member of the cloth participates in a sexual experience that is not prescribed by the tenets of his or her faith, a strong and convincing rationale must be provided for the behavior.

The Italian Pope was suffering from psychogenic blindness. Eminent authorities gathered from all over the world to try to cure him. After intensive examination the group advised him that they knew of only one cure. "Pontiff, you must have sexual intercourse." Though the Pope was taken aback, he decided to cooperate with their recommendation for the good of his flock. "But there have to be several conditions! One, the woman musta be blindafolded. Second, the woman cannota be Roman Catholic. Three, this cannota take-a place in Roma, Italy." The doctors assured the Pope these conditions could be met, and as they were leaving, the Pope called out, "One-a last thing. Make-a sure she's got-a bigga tits."

Not only must clergymen refrain from many kinds of sexual experiences, but they also have to be very careful of their language. Cursing is ungodly and a sin.

A priest and a minister were playing golf. The minister shanked the ball into the woods and blurted out, "Oh, shit!" The priest said he would not continue to play golf in the presence of such language. The minister apologized and said it would not happen again. But when his ball plopped into a water hazard, again he exclaimed, "Oh, shit!" This time the priest gathered his clubs and prepared to leave, remaining only after the minister profusely apologized and said, "May God strike me dead if I say that again." They continued playing until the minister missed an easy putt, when he said, "Oh, shit" again. There was

thunder from heaven, a flash of lightning, and the priest
instead of the minister was struck dead, and a deep voice
from heaven exclaimed, "Oh, shit!"

Despite the worldly interests that occasionally break
through, a religious leader is supposed to be humble and not
seek to enhance himself. This is often too much to ask of any
mortal even if he or she is a devout servant of God.

A very revered rabbi was being introduced by a member of
the board who was extremely laudatory and eloquent in
his remarks. "We are about to hear from a man of such
wisdom that even the most learned worship him, of such
kindness that children of all ages seek him out for counsel,
with such profound insight into human problems that men
and women share their innermost thoughts, a man of
such . . . " At this point the rabbi tugged at the orator's
sleeve and whispered, "Don't forget my humility."

Rabbis and other clergymen often are asked to be psychotherapists.

A congregant approached the rabbi and told him business
was bad, his wife was leaving him, his children were
terrible. The rabbi said, "I don't have the answer to
everything, so go home, open the Bible and wherever your
finger lands, there will be the answer to your plight." The
man followed the rabbi's prescription and a few weeks
later sought out the rabbi to tell him, "Rabbi, you are a
genius. You solved all my problems. I went home, opened
the Bible and there was the answer to all my problems."
"Where did it land?" the rabbi asked with much curiosity.
The man answered, "Chapter Eleven."

Similarities and Differences

Adherents of religious faiths are constantly trying to buttress
their own positions. Many jokes deal with proponents of a

religion lauding their own way of life and questioning the practices of other faiths. Latent competition is obviously an issue in these jokes reflecting the enmity of the major and minor religions toward each other.

> Question: What is the difference between Christians and Jews. Answer: At the end of a party, Christians leave but they don't say goodbye. Jews say goodbye but they don't leave.

At most places of worship, congregants give money to keep the institution financially solvent. In churches this is often a ritual on Sunday mornings when they pass the plate. In synagogues, often on the Day of Atonement congregants make pledges of future contributions.

> Mr. Isadore Cohen arose during services at the appropriate time to make his financial pledge. "I am from the haber-dashery store of I. Cohen. We are at 732 Delancey Street. We are open every day from 8:30 A.M. to 8:00 P.M. except on the Sabbath and on Jewish holidays. We sell suits, ties, and shirts at a good price. Our phone number is 620–4136. My partner and I would like to pledge $500 anonymously."

> There was a robbery at the local synagogue the day after Yom Kippur and it was reported that $30,000 in pledges were stolen.

Of all the religious groups, the Jews are particularly known for their ethnic pride. According to them, anybody who is Jewish is a special person, a member of the tribe, an integral part of God's chosen people. There are many jokes that contain the theme of Jewish ethnocentrism, affording both Jews and Gentiles the opportunity to mock this form of defensive arrogance.

Little Jake ran into the house and shook his grandfather who was napping. "Grandpa, Grandpa, the Yankees beat Chicago 7–2." The grandfather opened his eyes and asked, "Is that good for the Jews?"

Mrs. Horowitz was vacationing at a Jewish hotel and saw the famous singer, Perry Como, in the dining room. She went over to him and asked, "Mr. Como, tell me, are you Jewish?" Perry Como politely answered, "No, I'm not." Mrs. Horowitz still wondered, and when she saw Perry during the day, at the pool, at the golf course, she kept asking him, "Are you Jewish?" For the umpteenth time she approached him asking, "Mr. Como, are you sure you're not Jewish?" Finally irritated, Perry Como answered, "Yes, I am!" Mrs. Horowitz responded, "Funny, you don't look it."

Two Jewish men had just come from Pincus, the tailor, and as they were walking down the street, Itzak turned to his friend and said, "Our new suits fit fine, but as I look at yours and mine, I'm not sure they're really black. They might be navy blue." "You're right, they do sort of look navy blue but it's hard to tell. I wouldn't want to be seen in anything but black!" "I have an idea," said Itzak. "We're approaching that convent, and we could compare our suits with the nuns' habits since they only wear black." His friend agrees, and they ring the convent bell. A nun comes to the door and they have a brief interchange. The Mother Superior comes to the nun to ask who that was at the door. "I don't know," says the nun, "but they were two learned men." "How do you know that?" the Mother Superior wanted to know. "Well," said the nun, "they spoke Latin. They said, 'Pincus Fuctus.'"

Although fostering group belongingness is important to many groups, there is ambivalence attached to the activity.

Mrs. Feldman got on the bus and in Yiddish asked, "*Ret Yiddish?*" [Do you speak Yiddish?] of a passenger who

shook his head. Mrs. Feldman went to three other passen-
gers, asking them, *"Ret Yiddish?"* without an affirmative
answer. Finally one man answered "Yes." To him she said,
"Vot time is it?"

In twentieth century America, people of different races and
religions work together to try to achieve more harmonious
relationships. In the process, many truths are revealed. Several
of the interdenominational and interracial jokes are attempts to
deal with the differences between groups and laugh at them,
rather than fight about them.

A priest and a rabbi were together enjoying the boxing
matches at Madison Square Garden. One of the fighters
crossed himself before the opening gong. "What does that
mean?" the rabbi asked. The priest replied, "Not a damn
thing if he can't fight."

Mr. Goldberg shared a table in the ship's dining room with
a Frenchman and neither could speak the other's language.
When the Frenchman arrived at the table, bowed and said,
"Bon appetit," Mr. Goldberg bowed and responded,
"Goldberg." This ritual went on at their table each meal for
a week. Finally another passenger explained to Mr. Goldberg that the Frenchman wasn't telling his name, but was
wishing Goldberg a good appetite. At the next meal, Mr.
Goldberg smiled at the Frenchman, bowed and said, "Bon
appetit." The Frenchman smiled, bowed, and said, "Goldberg."

When a young Jewish man fell in love with a Native
American woman and wanted to marry her, his family
disowned him and they did not speak for a few years.
When his wife was pregnant, the son called his father and
thought he could reestablish a relationship. "Papa, you're
going to be a grandfather." The grandfather-to-be sounded
softer and willing to talk. "And Papa, you'll be pleased,

we're giving the baby a Jewish name." "What name?" he
wants to know. "Whitefish."

Fostering smoother relationships among different ethnic,
religious, and racial groups begins in childhood.

A teacher, working on an international relations project,
asked the class, "Who can tell me where the Russian
border is?" A student responded, "In the park with my
aunt, and my mother doesn't trust him."

Interfaith and interracial get-togethers lead to all kinds of
complications. Woody Allen recalls, "My parents sent me to an
interfaith camp where I was beaten up by boys of all races and
religions."

Father O'Clancy walked into a haberdashery with a sign on
it, Greenberg and O'Sullivan. He was greeted by a bearded
man wearing a yarmulke [a skull cap worn by religious
Jews]. "Well sir," smiled Father O'Clancy, "I jist want ye
t'know how good it is for an Irishman like me to see your
people and mine working together as partners. It's a foine
s'prise!" "Father, I thank you, but I'll give you a better
surprise," said the bearded man. "I'm O'Sullivan."

Competition Always Rears Its Head

Despite efforts to bring people of different races or religions
together, the differences seem to be accentuated by some.
Particularly, religious leaders seem to worry that their group
will be obliterated if they do not constantly assert the differences between themselves and others.

Said the rabbi to the priest, "You'll go back to your church
and worship God in your way." Then he said to the
minister, "And you'll go back to your church and worship

God in your way." And then the rabbi concluded, "And I'll go back to my synagogue and worship God in *His* way!"

A rabbi and a priest were in a serious car accident. As they lay on the ground in pain, the priest crossed himself, whereupon the rabbi went through the same motions. The priest commented, "Rabbi, I see you are fundamentally a good Catholic. You just crossed yourself." "Oh, no," said the rabbi. "After an accident like this, I make a checkup." Pointing down toward his crotch and up to his eyes he says, "Testicles, spectacles." Moving his arm left and then right across his chest, "wallet and watch."

Hymie Cohen, while crossing the street, was knocked down in front of a church. The priest came out to comfort him, and out of habit said, "My child, do you believe in God the Father, God the Son, and God the Holy Ghost?" Cohen murmurs, "Here I am dying and he asks riddles!"

Very often religious groups compete to determine who has purer attitudes toward sexuality.

A young lady went to a Roman Catholic church to confess that she had premarital sexual relations. Although the priest was ready to listen, when the young lady also confessed that the sex was conducted on a chandelier, the priest told her she was a pervert and told her to leave. The lady then went to a Protestant house of worship and told the minister about her premarital sexual relations on a chandelier, and the minister's reaction was similar to the priest's. He told the woman she was a sinner and he could not help her. Finally she visited a rabbi who cordially invited her to have a glass of tea. She was very impressed by the rabbi's hospitality and went on to tell him that she had been ejected from both a Catholic and Protestant church for sexual improprieties. She told him about her sex on a chandelier. The rabbi smiled benignly and com-

mented, "What do these Gentiles know about fancy fucking?"

I think it was Amanda Smith of the Scripps Howard News
Service who suggested that ethnic jokes start as a means for
powerful people to belittle a minority group by sneering at a
caricature of them. However, if the minority group gains
strength and self-confidence it may adopt the ethnic joke for
itself, as an "in-joke" to be told only by group members. This
has certainly been true of the many jokes that Jews tell about
other Jews.

> Ginsberg is telling his good friend a joke. "One day these
> two Jewish guys—" His friend stops him and asks indig-
> nantly, "Why are your jokes always about Jews? Why
> don't you talk about another group for a change!" "Okay,"
> says Ginsberg, "one day these two Chinese guys go into a
> synagogue with their prayer shawls and yarmulkes on
> because it was their niece's Bat Mitzvah . . . "

Jews compete with each other about many issues—religious
ideology, rituals, and family life. There are many jokes involving their infighting that they like to tell about themselves
to each other.

> An Orthodox, Conservative, and Reform Jew are arguing
> about the merits of their respective houses of worship. The
> Orthodox Jew says, "Every Saturday morning we have the
> most dignified Sabbath service that you can imagine.
> Everybody is elegantly dressed and you can hear a pin
> drop during the service—the decorum is just magnificent."
> The Conservative Jew remarks, "We have the most won-
> derful Sabbath services, the music is the best, the rabbi is
> a tremendously eloquent orator, and the morale of our
> congregation can't be beat." The Reform Jew comments,
> "We have wonderful dancing at our Temple every Friday
> night, the liquor flows, and we have the best poker games.

On the New Year and on the Day of Atonement, drive by and see the gorgeous sign on our Temple in neon lights, 'Closed for the High Holy Days.'"

A Jewish lady who was considering the possibility of assimilating with non-Jews went to visit her Orthodox rabbi to get a *b'rucha* [blessing] for a Christmas tree. The rabbi told her Jews do not celebrate Christmas so he could not supply her with a *b'rucha*. The lady then visited a Conservative rabbi with the same request. He told her that although he admired her liberal attitude, he could not endorse the practice of Jews having Christmas trees and he could not bless the event. As a last resort the lady visited a Reform rabbi asking for a *b'rucha* for a Christmas tree. He nodded, "I can get you a Christmas tree, but what the hell is a *b'rucha*?"

On a cold winter night, Mr. Liebowitz, a devout Orthodox Jew, feeling his time had come, called to his wife, "Faygele, please send someone to the temple and get the Reform rabbi, Rabbi Berk, and tell him to come right away because I am dying." "A Reform rabbi? Are you absolutely crazy? Have you gone mad? You mean you want our own rabbi, Rabbi Abramowitz!" declared his anxious wife. "Why," she wanted to know, "would you insist on a Reform rabbi?" "Why disturb our revered Rabbi Abramowitz on a cold winter night like this?"

Catholics sometimes like to joke about themselves, too.

Mr. Frank Perdue, the renowned owner of the highly successful chicken business is alleged to have sent a deputy to Rome to make an important request. His Holiness was represented by a bishop who listened to the request, "We would like to have the Lord's prayer slightly modified. Instead of 'Give us this day our daily bread' we would like one word changed to make it 'our daily chicken.'" The two men discussed the proposition politely but the bishop was not convinced. Perdue's aide proposed, "We'll give the Vatican two million dollars a year if you go ahead with this." A few moments later His Holiness' aide was heard asking his assistant, "Could you review the Wonder Bread contract and let me know what it says?"

One of the Pope's assistants approached him and said, "Father, I regret to have to tell you this, but we have a case of genital herpes in the Vatican." "Good," replied His Holiness, "I'm getting tired of Soave Bolla."

One of the problems with ethnic jokes is that they reinforce stereotypes. We note they invariably contain many inconsistencies and opposites. For example, Jews are both monopolists and communists; WASPs are both timid and constricted on one hand, but arrogant and belligerent on the other. Italian Catholics are rigid and subordinate to religious doctrine but are also sexually free. Black men are supposed to spend all their time indulging their sexual passions, but are also considered to be disciplined athletes.

The current stereotype of Polish people is that they are intellectually limited. I have heard the following two jokes from a Polish colleague:

A fellow was telling jokes at a bar. He started, "There was this Polish guy . . . " but was interrupted by the bartender who angrily said, "Hey, I'm Polish, and the guy next to you is Polish, and the guy at that table is Polish." The joke teller responded, "Okay, then I'll tell the joke slowly."

A Polish man was thrilled to get a jigsaw puzzle for his birthday. He set all twelve pieces out on a card table and every day when he came home from his office he would work on it. One day he jumped up from the table and ran to the phone. "Stella," he cried, "you know that puzzle you gave me? Well, I finished it!" "Gee, Stanley, that's great," responded Stella hesitantly, "but did it take you all this time, three months, to finish the puzzle?" "Pretty good, eh?" Stanley said with some pride, "on the box it says 'Two to five years.'"

A couple of WASP stories:

Question: How can you tell it's a WASP in the shower? Answer: He gets out to pee.

Graffiti: WASPs make their money the old-fashioned way: They inherit it.

African-Americans have gained in self-esteem during the past two or three decades. The jokes they tell about themselves reflect their increased ability to take on the white majority's stereotypes about them.

Primrose had gone to elementary school in the South and moved to New York City when she was in her late teens. Ten years later her school chum came to visit. They reminisced on old times and caught up on the last ten years. When Primrose's 3-year-old came into the living room, Primrose said, "Tyrone, you can have milk and cookies now." When the 6-year-old came in, Primrose said, "Tyrone, how about drawing a picture for my friend." When her 9-year-old came home from school, Primrose said, "Tyrone, you better do your homework before you go out to play." Primrose's friend was puzzled. "How come all your children are named Tyrone? When you need them, how do they know it?" "Oh," Primrose explained, "then I call them by their last name."

Did you hear about the rural Mississippi elementary school's production of Snow White and the Seven Dwarfs? They had to bus in Snow White.

Passing and Failing

Members of minorities who have experienced a great deal of discrimination often identify with the aggressor (A. Freud 1946) and try to "pass." Instead of acknowledging their minority status, they try to pretend they are a member of the majority. But as clinicians know, the truth eventually emerges because to "pass" or deny one's racial or religious identity goes against superego commands and causes much guilt. When we feel guilty, we have a wish, albeit unconscious, to confess the truth. There are many stories about Jews who try to convert or pass, but they never quite fully succeed.

> Herman Rabinowitz opens a hardware store in a fancy neighborhood but few customers come. Very concerned about his investment, Herman consults a member of the Chamber of Commerce about the problem. The man is frank with Herman and says that the reason is probably because he is Jewish and people in that neighborhood don't want to patronize his store. "What should I do?" asks Herman. "The only thing I could suggest is to convert to Christianity." Herman thinks it over and decides, "Business is business." His training requires many rituals, memorizing parts of the New Testament, and the final requirement is to deliver a sermon in church on Sunday morning. He prepares carefully and standing before the church members he begins, "Fellow *goyim*." ["Fellow gentiles."]

> Sam Goldstein, a senior citizen, goes for a vacation in Miami. While touring the city, he sees an interesting edifice that turns out to be a Catholic church. After being shown around for an hour, he leaves after having been baptized. He calls up his wife to tell her, but she is on her way to a canasta game and tells him she has no time to talk to him now. He then calls his son, an attorney, who is too busy with a client to talk to his father. His daughter puts

him off also. Sam reflects to himself, "I've been a *goy*
[Gentile] for 20 minutes and already there are three Jews I
don't like."

Hymie Cohen changed his name to Harrison Cole and
opened a jewelry business. His sale of crucifixes was so
lucrative that he decided to sell them exclusively. He called
his distributor and asked for three hundred crosses. The
voice at the other end of the line asked, "You vant dem mit
duh Jesuses or mit out duh Jesuses?"

Members of minorities tend to ascribe all types of power to
the majority. Like children with adults, members of minority
groups distort the power that the majority possesses. Then
they believe that belonging to the restricted country club, the
anti-Semitic or anti-black swimming club, or the WASP sorority
or fraternity is a unique privilege that will bring them fame and
fortune.

Adele Horowitz changed her name to Del Hartley and
applied for membership to the Christian Ladies Golf Club.
She cleverly modified her credentials changing her religion, her educational background, and anything that
might make her appear Jewish. After she passes the
initiation rites, she is invited to a luncheon at the golf club
in honor of new members. Everything is going well and
she is starting to win friends and influence people. In the
middle of a conversation with the club president, she spills
a glass of water on the woman, puts her hand to her head
and exclaims, "*Oi vey is meer!*" [Oh woe is me!] When she
sees everyone at the table staring at her she adds, "Whatever that means."

Even when minority group members marry someone from
the majority, they are not exempt from discrimination.

Groucho Marx was married to a non-Jew. When their little
son was refused membership in a restricted country club,

Groucho sent the club a letter, "Inasmuch as my son is only half-Jewish, would it be permissible if he goes into the swimming pool only up to his waist?"

Max Markowitz changes his name to Michael Monroney and applies to an elite, anti-Semitic golf club. He is granted an interview and is asked if he plays golf. Faking a Harvard accent he declares, "I have considerable expertise in the sport." His interviewer is impressed and asks what he does for a living. Ex-Max replies, "I participate in horse trading and my avocation is commercial real estate." When ex-Max is about to be accepted into the club, he is asked his religion. "My religion? Why, I'm a *goy!*"

During the last three decades there have been more inter-marriages and conversions than at any other time in American history. Rabbis, priests, and ministers have been very upset about the number of adherents leaving their fold.

Said a rabbi to a minister as he was bemoaning the loss of congregants to other faiths, "Some of my best Jews are Friends."

In this day and age of conversions and "passing," interesting complications can result.

In a Jewish restaurant, a customer is greeted by a Chinese waiter who speaks Yiddish beautifully. When the man is paying his bill to the restaurant owner he asks, "Where did you get a Chinese waiter who knows Yiddish?" "Shh," the owner says, "he thinks he's learning English."

Can You Top This?

When I was about 12 years old, I listened every week to a radio program called "Can You Top This?" On the program, four expert joke tellers would relate stories and jokes on designated topics. A laugh meter measuring the audience's response was used to determine who told the funniest joke on the topic. At the time I routinely listened to the program, I was also trying to cope better with the enormous amount of anti-Semitism that I experienced during most of my youth in Canada. As I reviewed the many verbal and physical fights I had, I began to refer to the "one-upmanship" fracases as similar to "Can You Top This?" Despite the many attempts that we all make to love rather than hate and to cooperate rather than compete, religious and racial hatred persists. There are certain jokes that reflect the intense and persistent hatred between various groups.

> During a tour of Jerusalem while the guide was showing off Israel to the tourists, a fellow in the crowd yelled out, "Fuck Golda Meir!" The guide tried to ignore the boorish fellow, but the provocateur persisted, "Fuck Golda Meir!" The guide finally said, "Hey, you are debasing our Prime Minister! Cut it out." But the brash fellow continued, "Fuck Golda Meir." The guide then angrily asked the man, "Where are you from?" He replied, "Ireland." "Ireland, huh?" the guide reflected. "Well then, fuck Ella Fitzgerald."

I remember this joke from World War II and frequently tell it because it gratifies many of my revengeful fantasies toward bigots.

> During World War II, a lady from the deep South calls the local army base and tells the sergeant, "We would like to extend an invitation to our home to five enlisted men for Thanksgiving dinner." "That's very kind of you ma'am," says the sergeant. "Just please make sure that not one of them is Jewish." The sergeant arranges to send five soldiers over to the woman's home. When she goes to the door to greet the soldiers, she becomes acutely upset. She

finds five black soldiers standing in front of her. One of the enlisted men greets her and says, "We are here for the Thanksgiving dinner, ma'am." The woman with obvious rancor in her voice says, "Your sergeant has made an error!" "Oh, no, ma'am," the soldier replies, "Sergeant Cohen never makes an error!"

As Freud (1937b) so often said, "Although we all make attempts to do so, it remains difficult to 'love thine enemy' and 'turn the other cheek.'"

A little Jewish man gets on an airplane and is seated next to a Texan twice his size who is already fast asleep. As the plane takes off the little Jewish man gets airsick and vomits all over the Texan. After awhile the Texan opens his eyes and sees the mess on himself. The little Jewish man looks at him empathetically and asks, "You feel better now?"

A Jewish man is on the subway reading the Yiddish newspaper *The Forward*. An anti-Semite sits down next to him and in an aggressive manner pointing to a column in the paper bellows, "What does dat say?" The Jewish man answers, "Syphilis." Then the man points to another spot on the paper and again asks, "What does dat say!?" The Jewish man answers, "Gonorrhea." "And what does dat say?," asks the anti-Semite once more. The Jew answers, "Clap." "And dat?" asks the man again. The Jew reading the paper says, "The Pope is very sick."

Even the elegant and erudite attempt to top each other. Bigotry does not seem to be a stranger to any social, economic, religious, racial, or political group.

At an elegant dinner party, a very wealthy gentleman who was also a vicious anti-Semite, was describing a trip to Africa. "It was wonderful," he commented, "I didn't run into a single pig or a single Jew." A hush fell over the table and then the voice of a Jewish guest was heard, "What a shame. The two of us could have corrected that so easily." "Oh, how come?" asked the wealthy gentleman. Replied the Jewish guest, "We could have gone there together."

An arrogant English lord known for his anti-Semitism asked Chaim Weizmann, then the President of Israel, "Weizmann, can you tell me why it is that you Jews are reputed to be so mercenary?" Weizmann replied, "For the same reason, m'lord, that you English are said to be gentlemen."

Writers who have presented jokes on racial and religious matters, for example Rosten (1985) and Telushkin (1992), remind us that many members of minorities are acutely sensitive to accents, dialects, and hearing their group derided. It is often difficult for many of us to cope with both the affectionate feeling that should be part of any joke and the latent derision that is also frequently present. This is a difficult task particularly when it comes to exchanging ethnic stories. I find Leo Rosten's (1985) remarks about this issue most soothing and salutary.

The laughter of a people can be as illuminating as its patterns of pride, guilt, and shame. I think humor is an isotope that locates the values of a culture. The japery of a nation runs up and down the scale of its scorn and its admiration, its approval or contempt.

Any collection of ethnic jokes is, perforce, a parade of its heroes, patsies, wise men, clowns. The particular genius, or inherent limitations, of any group beholden to the same preferences and taboos is as much revealed by a sampling of its humor as by a sampling of its IQs, indeed more so, I submit, since the IQ protocol tests only a certain kind of intelligence; it reveals nothing about humor, judgment, affability. God preserve us from those who have no sense of humor, for they are the scourges of humankind. [p. 7]

6

Jewish Doctors Afraid of the Sight of Blood: Psychotherapists and Psychotherapy

No vocation or profession evokes as much emotion in its protagonists or antagonists as does psychotherapy. Patients fear and criticize it, non-patients scorn and demean it, and therapists try to defend and protect it. Like religion, different "schools" compete against each other, vying to have a monopoly on the psychological truth and helping people make the most constructive changes.

The warring factions within the mental health professions have brought each other to court, and it is not unknown for some members of one psychoanalytic society to split and sue the others for professional improprieties. Accusations of malpractice by patients, families, and communities have been widespread during the past two decades. A month does not go by without a newpaper headline accusing a psychotherapist of being a charlatan.

Whenever there is intense affect about a phenomenon, there are usually many factors at work that contribute to all the excitement. Why does psychotherapy arouse so much hatred, scorn, and cynicism?

Sometimes it is easy for us who live in the 1990s to overlook the fact that psychotherapy, as it is practiced today, is little more than one hundred years old. If we consider the number of centuries that human beings have been trying to cope with their internal and external lives, psychotherapy, as a profession designed to help them cope, is in its infancy. The idea that men, women, and children have difficulties in loving themselves and others, that they cannot deal with their aggressive and sexual drives efficiently, are unsure of their roles in the family, at work, and in the community, but do have a legitimate right to be helped with these problems, is a revolutionary idea (Freud 1937b). For countless centuries, those who suffered from neurotic and psychotic difficulties were incarcerated in prisons, chained in shackles, and often physically beaten. To suffer from emotional distress was tantamount to a crime (DeMause 1982).

Unfortunately, the punitive attitude toward sufferers of psychic turmoil has not been completely eradicated. In a society that champions notions like autonomy and independence, the idea of seeking out another person to help alleviate one's emotional troubles is still experienced all too frequently as a sign of weakness (Strean 1991). We are now living in an era when many mental health professionals are preferring drugs to treat mental stress. In some ways we are returning to the old days when the one-to-one therapist–patient relationship so necessary for the proper conduct of psychotherapy is bypassed. To ask for therapeutic help is still not easy for most, to view it as a constructive and mature step appears foolhardy to many, and the way to achieve therapeutic success is still very much debated among professionals.

Although it is now recognized that individuals have much difficulty asking for therapeutic help and experience even more conflict while they receive it, if they do summon up the courage to seek out a therapist, there are still numerous difficulties for them to contend with. The mental health "industry" has been and continues to be organized so that those who need the most therapeutic help get the least assistance and the least trained helpers. A single woman living with numerous children, on welfare, overwhelmed, depressed by many internal and external burdens, if fortunate, might receive weekly therapy at a low-cost mental health center from a social worker with about two years experience. By contrast, someone with many more economic, social, and psychological resources can receive five-times-a-week analysis from a professional with many years of experience. The mental health professions still have a tendency to take flight from our patients, forcing those who need a great deal of therapeutic help to receive limited care, both in quality and quantity.

Psychotherapists are recipients of enormous criticism. How much of it is legitimate and how much is not? It is easy enough to assert that those who seek therapeutic help are ashamed of the idea; consequently, they knock their helpers to protect themselves. Feeling small and weak, they "shrink" those who treat. It is also easy enough to aver that psychotherapists who expose painful truths about human beings are inevitably going to be despised. We clinicians who confront people with their murderous wishes, incestuous fantasies, and homosexual and bisexual propensities are not going to be praised for doing so — we're more likely to be buried!

Although perceptions of psychotherapists are distorted, there is now a body of evidence to suggest that psychotherapists as a group are no less emotionally disturbed than are their patients and clients (Strean 1993, Sussman 1992). Yet, it is only within recent years that psychotherapists have been able to acknowledge that they form neurotic counterresistances and countertransferences as much as, if not more than, their patients form neurotic resistances and transferences. It is also only within the last several years that psychotherapists are more willing to move away from the antiquated medical model in which the wise and "together" doctor treats the naïve, disoriented patient. Clinicians have shown a great deal of resistance to accepting the fact that all of us, patients and therapists, are more human than otherwise. By this we mean mental disturbance is always a matter of degree—the differences between the psychotic man or woman in a mental hospital and the individual functioning outside of an institution are less than the similarities. What the "normal" person dreams at night, the psychotic person fantasies during the day (Fine 1985, Strean 1991, 1993).

One of the most serious and unresolved issues in psychotherapy is the enormous antagonism among mental health professionals. For many decades competition was severe between medical and nonmedical therapists. Although this has eased somewhat, practitioners with different theoretical orientations have much reluctance to listen to each other, and proponents of one modality tend to look at those who prefer another as second-class citizens! Advocates of brief treatment tend to disparage long-term treatment and vice versa. Behaviorists usually loathe those who endorse dynamic psychotherapy and vice versa. Within psychoanalysis, battles wage more vociferously and intensely between "schools" than are those fought out by religious sects. Self psychologists and the "object relations" advocates are convinced that "classical" analysts or those who endorse "drives" are passé. Classical analysts, of course, do not show great tolerance toward their dissenters either. For some psychoanalysts, if a patient is seen four times a week, it is considered ipso facto "psychoanalysis"; if the frequency is three times a week and the one who conducts it does not call it psychotherapy, he or she is, for sure, a heretic and/or not a "psychoanalyst."

All of these aforementioned issues may help us appreciate a little more why psychotherapy is mocked so frequently. It is still not completely acceptable to be in psychotherapy in the 1990s. For example, George Bush during his 1992 presidential campaign referred to those who wish to examine their conflicts, fantasies, and dreams in a psychotherapist's office as "cowards." Yet, though the numbers who deplore psychotherapy keep increasing, more individuals keep seeking therapeutic help. Yes, there is still much intense ambivalence toward it!

Because of the ambivalence toward psychotherapy by many and the anxiety it induces in most, jokes proliferate on the subject. As I have studied the many stories and anecdotes about psychotherapy, they can be divided into a few categories. There are jokes about "crazy" patients. There are other jokes about "crazy" therapists. Therapeutic techniques are also the object of mockery as is the entire therapeutic process. In recent years, there have been a few jokes on self-help procedures in psychotherapy, implying that individuals who want to be helped therapeutically might be better off ministering to themselves. Let us consider some of the anecdotes about the consumers of psychotherapy, people called "patients," or "clients," or sometimes "customers."

The Consumers

One of the greatest fears noted among those who seek psychotherapy is "going crazy." Usually this means experiencing a psychotic episode whereby all of one's id wishes will erupt and the individual will want to act out forbidden sexual and aggressive impulses. I believe that this fear covers a wish to regress and become a baby. It is not easy for patients and non-patients who, as a rule, value independence, initiative, and autonomy, to accept a wish to be an infant. Instead, they mock those who more openly show their infantilism, such as those who are diagnosed as schizophrenics.

Joking about schizophrenia and other mental illnesses is probably a more benign way of dealing with our anxiety about becoming psychotic than it is to imprison psychotic patients or to hit them over the head and call it shock therapy. It is also a little less sadistic to single out a mental patient and joke about him, therefore diminishing some of our own concerns about being singled out as a disturbed person, than it is to isolate a helpless and troubled person and keep him or her locked up in a closed ward. A poem, recited to me by an outpatient of mine, deals with this issue.

> Roses are red,
> Violets are blue,
> I'm schizophrenic,
> And so am I.

This non-rhyme reveals the antiquated notion that schizophrenia means split personality—one minute the person is Dr. Jekyll and the next Mr. Hyde. What this perspective overlooks is that all of us enact different roles and show different degrees of maturity at different times and in different social contexts. We all manifest different ego states depending on where we are and with whom. The split personality notion of schizophrenia ignores the fact that the person suffering from it finds reality horrifying and therefore regresses to the behavioral modes of a child. A better way of defining schizophrenia might be "a regression in ego functioning."

One of the problems with diagnostic categories is that they fail to individualize patients. There is a broad range of individuals with unique behavior and symptoms that can be placed under one diagnostic umbrella.

The following poem may be an excellent substitute for *DSM-III* (*Diagnostic and Statistical Manual III*), a manual that tends to pigeonhole specimens who are not pigeons!

> Neuroses are red,
> Depression is blue.
> I'm schizophrenic,
> How about you?

In certain types of mental disturbance the individual refuses to talk. Usually this man, woman, or child profoundly distrusts his or her fellow human beings so much that a complete withdrawal from them seems to be the safest protective measure.

> Two patients in a mental hospital sat next to each other on a bench in complete silence for hours. One day during the fourth week of their hospital stay, after sitting silently for three and a half hours, one of them blurted out, "Oy." The other replied, "You're telling *me*?"

This joke suggests that if defenses are supported and the mental patient is not forced to talk, he feels safer and becomes more "object related." Many inpatient as well as outpatient facilities believe that "a patient should be met where he is"— nothing should be imposed on him or her too quickly. With this in mind, the patient can make steady progress, eventually return to his or her previous way of life. However, it is not simple to get discharged from a mental hospital.

> The phone rang at the nurse's desk in Ward Eight of the mental hospital. "Can you tell me how Abraham Cohen is getting along?" The nurse consulted her chart and said, "Just fine. The psychiatrist said he can go home on Tuesday. Who shall I say called him?" "No one. I'm Cohen. That psychiatrist treats me like a *meshugeneh* [crazy one] and won't tell me a damn thing."

I believe the paranoid patient is the butt of many jokes because in paranoia we project onto others our own forbidden wishes and punitive superego commands. Therefore paranoia is something "familiar" (Freud 1908, Reik 1962) to us. We all have wishes that we prefer to ascribe to others and at the same time do not like to believe we are projecting. Most of us like to consider ourselves responsible and insightful mature adults.

Psychotherapists have recognized for some time that many individuals, perhaps most, find it difficult to accept their own homosexual fantasies. These wishes, perhaps more than other desires, are projected onto others.

> A patient in psychotherapy is reported to have told his therapist, "I've just flown to New York, and when I went through Immigration they asked me if I was gay. I said, 'No, but I've slept with a lot of guys who are.'"

> A prospective patient was given some projective tests. The first card consisted of two vertical lines. "What do you see?," asked the psychologist. "I see two men standing up having sex with each other." To the next card of two horizontal lines, the man responded, "Here are two men, having anal intercourse." Then a card of two circles was presented and to this the would-be patient commented, "I see two obese men having sex." The man was taken into treatment and after about three weeks he notified his therapist, "I'm going to a stag party in a few days. Could I borrow those dirty pictures you showed me a few weeks ago?"

As time passes, some patients are more willing to face their paranoid mechanisms.

> Said one man who had been in treatment several months, "I am less afraid of 'the woman' in me. Now I can treat women more as my equal. I am not as sexist. Of course, most women don't like to be treated like a paranoid, balding, obese man with contact lenses."

> It may have been the same patient who defined a musician as a man who, hearing a female singing in the shower, put his ear to the keyhole.

Patients do begin to accept the notion that mental distur-bance is a matter of degree and that there are not such major differences between neurotics, psychotics, and "normal" people. Some definitions:

> A psychotic thinks that two plus two equals nine; a neurotic knows perfectly well that two plus two equals four—but he just cannot accept the fact. . . .

> A neurotic builds castles in the air, the psychotic lives in them, and the psychotherapist collects rent from both.

Dale Carnegie, in his book *How to Win Friends and Influence People*, defined a neurotic as a person who when asked, "How are you?" tells you.

Behind paranoia and other forms of distorted thinking are grandiose fantasies. All of us would like to be kings, queens, princes, or princesses. This universal narcissism (Freud 1914) is easier to laugh at in others than to accept in ourselves. My favorite story on grandiosity comes from Leo Rosten's (1985) *Giant Book of Laughter*.

> "Sit down, Mr. Pelham," said the psychiatrist. "Now, what brings you here?" "People!," declared Pelham. "Stupid people! Doctor, I have to tell you I despair about the whole human race!" "Mmmh. Well what is it that people actually do that makes you so bitter?" "They call me crazy, that's what they do! No matter what I say or suggest—they say I am crazy! They won't listen to a word of truth!" "Mr. Pelham," said the psychiatrist gently, "perhaps you ought to start at the beginning. . . . " Mr. Pelham said, "Okay. In the beginning, I created the heavens and the earth. And the earth was without form and void. . . . " [p. 407]

As clinicians have learned, some patients are aware of their grandiose wishes but they can't monitor them too well.

Mr. Gerald Stevens entered the therapist's office and when asked what was bothering him, told the therapist, "You see, I have this strong belief that I am the most beautiful horse in the world and everybody who observes me is smitten with my extreme beauty." The therapist asked, "Are you a female horse or a male horse?" Stevens got up and in a rage left the office saying, "I'm a male horse, you dope. What do you think, I've got problems with my gender identity?"

Sometimes one can have the delusion of being an object.

Mrs. Cornwall visited a therapist's office to report that her husband believed he was a refrigerator. The therapist was puzzled and asked for more information. Mrs. Cornwall said, "The guy sleeps with his mouth wide open." The therapist tried to convince Mrs. Cornwall that this was not an unusual symptom. "Many men sleep with their mouths open," he patiently advised. "But," retorted Mrs. Cornwall, "I can't get any sleep with that little light on all night."

Despite the fact that these days schizophrenia is better understood by both professionals and the lay community, not everyone has discarded the notion of the "split personality."

A patient entered a psychiatrist's office and reported, "I have the strong conviction that I am not one person, but two! I believe I'm two separate people. Am I going psychotic? Do you think I should start intensive treatment Doctor? . . . " "Just a moment," replied the doctor, "not so quickly. Begin from the beginning—and one at a time please."

Although therapists are trained to recognize that beneath manifest complaints are unconscious wishes, defenses, and superego commands that should be exposed, presenting prob lems like manifest dreams can nonetheless appear eerie and puzzling.

> Ms. Rhoda Moore consulted a therapist and began, "This is not my idea. My family doctor insisted I consult you. I really don't know why he was so insistent. I'm happily married, I have a good sex life, my children are healthy and happy, I have good friends." "Stop!" the therapist said with a concerned look on his face. "How long has this been going on?"

> Matt Green, a man in his fifties, went for a consultation because his memory was failing him. He told the therapist, "I meet people and I forget their names. I have to be at a certain place, and the appointment slips my mind. My wife asks me to run an errand and I don't remember where to go." With empathetic concern, the therapist inquired, "How long have you had this problem?" Matt hesitated and then asked, "What problem?"

As was said previously, in psychotherapy the units of diagnosis and treatment have been enlarged. Consequently, clinicians will often have consultations with members of the identified patient's family.

> Mrs. Hale visited a therapist, Dr. Lila Morton, to discuss her son. She told Dr. Morton that her son David was compulsively making mud pies. Dr. Morton explained, "That's no cause for alarm, Mrs. Hale. Making mud pies is developmentally appropriate and he will grow out of it." "I don't think so, " said Mrs. Hale. "His wife makes mud pies, too."

Psychotherapists have contended for some time that the mind and body are in a constant state of interaction. Psychological tensions can help bring on symptoms such as headaches and ulcers, and bodily conditions such as pneumonia can activate depression. As a result, practitioners get interesting requests.

> Mr. Stimson went to a psychotherapist for a consultation, pleading, "Doctor, please help me. Every morning at six o'clock I have to pass water and move my bowels." "What's wrong with that?" asked the therapist. "You see, Doctor, I don't get up until nine o'clock."

> Mr. Rabinowitz, a man in his eighties, suffered from severe insomnia. His children finally decided to bring him to a psychotherapist who specialized in treating insomniacs. Rather than use talk therapy, the clinician administered hypnosis. Mr. Rabinowitz agreed to come into the consulting room if his children accompanied him. Once Rabinowitz was seated comfortably, the therapist held up a watch and swung it back and forth. He said to Rabinowitz, "Your eyes are getting tired. You are becoming more relaxed. You are sleeping now." When the therapist saw that Mr. Rabinowitz's eyes were shut and his breathing had become more rhythmic, he placed his fingers on his lips cautioning Rabinowitz's children to be quiet. Then the therapist left the room for a moment, whereupon Rabinowitz opened one eye and asked, "That *meshugeneh* [crazy one], has he gone yet?"

Insomnia is a frequent presenting problem. A colleague told me she had a patient with a severe case of insomnia who complained to her, "Every time I fall asleep, I have a dream I'm awake."

Another colleague of mine told me about a patient who saw a headline in a newspaper, "Man Wanted for Armed Robbery in the Bronx." He told his therapist, "If that job was in Brooklyn, I'd take it."

Sometimes people in executive positions recognize the ability of psychotherapy to contribute to the well-being of their organizations by resolving problems in communication among their staff.

> A ship's captain, who was consulting a therapist to improve his handling of the large number of men under his command, told his therapist about having heard over the loudspeaker, "Now hear this, now hear this. Midshipman Gillespie, your father has died." He cringed to hear this insensitive announcement, and called in the radio operator. Explaining how someone might feel about such critical news, he said, "You need to be more gentle, not so abrupt. Find a kind way to inform someone about news like this." About a week later, he heard over the loudspeaker, "All hands on deck, all hands on deck." He watched the proceedings as the radio operator started by having the men stand at ease. Then the radio operator said, "All men whose mothers are alive, take one step forward." As most of the men started to take the step, he said, "Not so fast, Abercrombie. . . . "

Behavior modification has become a very popular form of therapy, particularly with children. Very often therapists instruct parents on how to reward, punish, and desensitize fears.

> Mrs. Lapidus consulted a behavioral therapist because her son Arthur got hysterical and screamed "Aiiii, *kreplach*!!" whenever she served *kreplach* [similar to a Chinese dumpling, usually served in soup]. After exploring the problem that was upsetting to Mrs. Lapidus, the therapist devised a program to desensitize Arthur. The idea was to show Arthur exactly how a *kreplach* is made. Mrs. Lapidus got Arthur to make dough with her, and roll it out on a board. "You're not frightened now, are you sweetheart?" Mrs. Lapidus said to her son. "No, Mama." She and Arthur cut out squares of dough and she again checked with him to see if he was afraid. "No, Mama." They chopped up meat with flavorings and again Arthur had no problem. Next they put a little mound of the meat into the center of each

square of dough. "Isn't this fun, Arthur? You're not frightened, are you?" All was well. Mrs. Lapidus folded over the first corner of the dough and Arthur did some with her. "No, Mama, I'm not frightened." Mrs. Lapidus pressed the second corner of the dough together and Arthur was still okay. Then she pressed the third corner down and was asking Arthur, "Isn't this nice . . . " when Arthur started to scream hysterically, "Aiiii, *kreplach*!"

The Practitioner

Therapists take a great deal of criticism for many reasons. An often-used definition of a psychiatrist is "a Jewish doctor afraid of the sight of blood." The definition really knocks the guy who's a dropout from the general practice of medicine because he's phobic. The fact that he's Jewish, thus maybe sort of a sissy, is implied, too. It expresses some of the hostility felt toward the doctor who will get to know all your problems, and refers to all psychotherapists, not just medically trained ones.

Almost every joke that deals with therapists as people has something negative to say about them. Even respectful and decent people have their angry feelings toward therapists. For twenty years at Rutgers University I had an excellent secretary who typed thousands of pages. She made two slips. When I suggested that "every social work student should have a parole case," she wrote "every student should have a pillow case." When I would dictate into the machine, "The therapist . . . " it came out "The rapist . . . "

The therapist is supposed to be a money grubber. Woody Allen, who spent many years as a patient in psychotherapy, said, "I was in analysis. I was suicidal. As a matter of fact I would have killed myself but I was in analysis with a strict Freudian and if you kill yourself they make you pay for the sessions you miss." And speaking of his therapist, he said, "Whenever I'm late, he begins without me."

Even therapists' children are critical of them.

> A daughter of a prominent woman psychoanalyst was
> asked what she'd like to be when she grew up. The
> daughter answered, "A patient." When asked why, she
> answered, "Then I'll see my Mommy at least four times a
> week."

> A woman analyst tried to answer her 4-year-old daughter's
> questions about where she was always going, "I have to
> see a patient." One day the confused child came into the
> waiting room, looked up at the next patient in the waiting
> room, and exclaimed, "Oh, you're not a patient, you're a
> person!"

Psychotherapists are frequently considered to be quite psychopathic and inhuman—the opposite of what they are supposed to be.

> A patient after several months of therapy said, "It must be
> difficult for you to listen to such horrible problems from so
> many people all day long." The therapist replied, "Who
> listens?"

> Another patient reported, "After twelve years in therapy,
> four times a week, my analyst finally said something that
> really got to me. He said, 'No hablo ingles.'"

> A patient told his friend, "Psychotherapists tell us one out
> of every five people is completely nuts." "Really?" said his
> friend. "Yeah, and you want to know the reason? Because
> the other four are not psychotherapists."

Jackie Mason in one of his humorous monologues captures
not only how psychopathic and devious therapists can be but
suggests how frightened prospective patients are of the proce-

dure. In *The Comedy Quote Dictionary*, Ronald Smith (1992) reproduces Mason's monologue on psychotherapy:

> I asked him, "What will this cost me?" He told me seventy-five dollars a visit. I said, "For seventy-five dollars, I don't visit, I move in." He said, "What's bothering you?" I said, "The seventy-five dollar fee for the visit." He said, "We have to search for the real you." I said to myself, "If I don't know who I am, how would I know what I look like? And even if I find me, how would I know it's me? Besides, if I want to look for me, why do I need him? I could look myself, or I could call my friends. They know where I've been! Besides, what if I find the real me, and I find that he's even worse than I am?" The psychiatrist said, "The search for the real you will continue at our next session. That will be seventy-five dollars." I said to myself, "This is not the real me. Why should I give him seventy-five dollars? What if I find the real me and he doesn't think it's worth seventy-five dollars? For all I know, the real me might be going to a different psychiatrist altogether. In fact, he might even be this psychiatrist himself!" I said to him, "What if you're the real me? Then you owe me seventy-five dollars." He said, "If you promise never to come back we'll call it even." [pp. 194–195]

> I was told that a psychoanalyst had a sign on his front door, "Three couches, no waiting."

During the last few years, therapists have been accused of exploiting their patients in many ways—sexually, economically, and interpersonally.

> Mr. Tom Nixon had been in therapy for four years and his therapist finally pronounced him cured of his kleptomania. As Mr. Nixon was leaving the therapist's office, he suggested, "Just to prove you've been cured, I want you to walk by Macy's on your way home and you'll see for yourself, you'll feel no temptation whatsoever to steal."

"Thank you very much! How can I show my profound appreciation to you?" asked Mr. Nixon. "Well," replied the therapist, "if you do regress, see if you can pick me up a color TV."

Therapeutic Procedures

Whenever people think of entering psychotherapy, they have all kinds of fantasies about what is going to happen to them. I've had patients tell me that I'm going to yell at them, criticize them, take their brains out, give them lobotomies, or rape them. Sometimes the fantasies are more benign: I might adopt them, marry them, feed them, tutor them, or have an affair with them. What patients fantasy will happen to them in therapy tells us a great deal about the child in them, and how that child influences their lives. I have found that each person, depending on what he or she fantasies will happen in and as a result of the therapy, has unique ideas about what the analytic couch is for. It can be everything from an operating table where drastic surgery will take place to a bed where pleasant love-making will occur. It can be a crib or a playpen, a coffin, or even a dungeon. There are many jokes that involve the couch, some of which we've already discussed, but a few more may be in order.

My late brother-in-law had a great joke for almost every occasion. (Many of the jokes in this book are ones he told me.) When I showed him my analytic office for the first time, he had many humorous things to say about the use of the couch:

A man enters an analyst's office for the first time. The analyst says, "The first thing I ask all my patients is what they do for a living." The man replies, "I'm an auto mechanic." The analyst then orders, "Get under the couch!"

A woman in intensive analysis says to her analyst, "I'd like just one kiss from you." The analyst replies, "Oh, no, that would interfere with the therapeutic process." "It won't hurt you, come on, kiss me!" When the lady persists, the analyst says, "I can't kiss you. I shouldn't even be on the couch with you."

My brother-in-law reeled off the next one:

A sexy woman enters an analyst's office for the first time. The analyst orders her to take off all her clothes and he does the same. He then gets on the couch with her and makes love. "We've taken care of my problem," says the analyst, "now, what's yours?"

Psychoanalytically oriented therapists encourage their patients to report their dreams and associate to the contents of the dream, thereby releasing repressed material. Although clinicians who use dreams in their work are admonished to wait for the patient to associate to the manifest content of dreams before offering interpretations, many therapists, particularly in this era of short-term treatment, become impatient.

A man entered an analyst's office and reported that he was suffering from a repetitive dream. "Each night I dream I'm driving an eighteen-wheeler truck from New York to Chicago, and I wake up each morning exhausted." The analyst said confidently, "That's easily cured. When you get to Pittsburgh, call me and I'll drive it the rest of the way." The patient returned the following week to report that, indeed, he was cured. The analyst's reputation for curing repetitive dreams brought him another patient who reported, "Each night I dream I'm with four voluptuous women who are all vying for my attention. I wake up exhausted." The analyst advised the patient, "When you are finished with two of the women, call me and I'll take care of the other two." The following week the same patient came in looking bleary-eyed and exhausted and reported no improvement. The analyst admonished him, "I told you to call me after you finished with two of the women." The patient protested, "I did! I did! But your phone service said you were in Pittsburgh!"

Dreams, as many clinicians and others know, contain universal symbols. Older people stand for parents; young people, for siblings; purses symbolize vaginas; ties can represent penises. Sometimes therapists are too eager to interpret the symbolic meaning of dreams before it is understood.

Jack Stone had a consultation with a fledgling analyst and told him about his repetitive dream. "Each night I dream I'm in a boat rowing in Central Park, when all of a sudden a powerful wind erupts. I lose one of my oars, and I wake up terrified, in a sweat." The young analyst gives an interpretation immediately, "Rowing in Central Park is having sex with your mother. The wind is your father who is angry with you, and the loss of your oar is the castration that you feel you deserve." Jack listened attentively to the analyst's remarks but never did return for another appointment. About two weeks later, Jack and the analyst happened to meet on the street and the analyst wanted to know why Jack had not come back to see him. "Well, things changed after I saw you. Now, in my nightly dream I'm having enjoyable sex with my mother, my father comes into the bedroom with an ax to castrate me, and I wake up in a sweat. But I tell myself, 'You're just rowing in Central Park.'"

Many psychotherapists were originally social workers. They have found that some of the procedures utilized in casework can have excellent effects.

Bob Brown, a social worker trained in psychoanalysis, is walking down the street carrying a couch on his back. A colleague he meets on the street wants to know where he's going carrying a couch. Bob explains, "I'm making a home visit."

When psychosomatic ills are treated in short-term therapy, the practitioner can offer interesting prescriptions.

> Mrs. Fink complains to her therapist, "I have this ringing in my ears." The therapist's solution: "Don't answer."

In the 1990s when therapists are permitting themselves to use countertransference reactions in the therapy, they sometimes carry things too far. For example, I have had colleagues tell me they have told boring patients to be more stimulating. I've even heard of some practitioners ending sessions before the time was up because the patient was not being productive.

> "Doctor," the patient complained, "why doesn't anyone pay any attention to me? My wife ignores me. My children never call me. I might as well not be in a room for all anyone notices me." The therapist was pensive for a brief moment, opened his door and called, "Next."

> Mr. Rhodes spent all his time in therapy talking about his "inferiority complex." His therapist listened session after session for years about his patient's conviction that he had an "inferiority complex." Finally the therapist notified Rhodes, "This will be your last session. I've discovered your problem. You *are* inferior!"

I have never met a therapist who did not have several patients who objected to the fee. It seems to me that this reflects patients' feelings that they do not get their money's worth. Many patients wish to be the therapist's friend, lover, spouse, or child and resent paying anything! When they see that the therapist makes a living from what seems to the patients to be simple human contact, they resent the clinician even more. Yet there are therapists who are too preoccupied with making a lot of money and do not sufficiently consider their patients' concerns.

Therapist: "My fee is two hundred dollars. That entitles you to three questions and answers." Patient, incredulously: "How much?" Therapist: "Two hundred dollars." Patient: "Isn't that a lot of money for three questions?" Therapist: "No, now what is your last question?"

One of the struggles between patient and therapist is that frequently patients want the treatment to be over quickly. Yet therapists try to train their patients to make no decisions in a hurry, but to examine in detail everything they feel, think, dream, or fantasy.

Selma Kates took her first vacation after being in intensive therapy for four years. She sent her therapist a postcard: "Hi. Having a wonderful time. Why?"

Patients and therapists have varied criteria to determine when therapy should end:

A 12-year-old thought he was ready to quit because "Now I can say 'shit' to my m-o-t-h-e-r."

Dr. Finley said to his patient, "Your analysis is now terminated. Doesn't that make you happy?" The patient responded , "I . . . I . . . I suppose so." Dr. Finley asked, "Why are you so hesitant? Do you remember how you felt when you first came to see me?" "Yes," said the patient, "much happier!"

Although therapists are instructed not to answer questions but to help the patient examine why he or she wants to ask a question, this precept is often violated.

A patient reported to this therapist about a very frustrating poker game he was in. "I lost a lot of money," lamented the patient and then described in obsessive detail how he played a particular hand. Then he asked, "How would you have played that hand, Doc?" The therapist replied, "Under an assumed name."

The idea of not answering patients' questions comes from the nondirective psychologist Carl Rogers, who believed in reflecting the patients' thoughts and feelings in a neutral manner, and nothing more.

Patient: "I'm feeling very bad." Therapist: "You're feeling bad." Patient: "My life has no meaning." Therapist: "You can't find meaning in your life." Patient: "I'm thinking of ending my life." Therapist: "You have a wish to terminate your existence." Patient: "I'm thinking of killing myself now." Therapist: "You have a desire to end your life instantly." The patient goes to the window, opens it, and jumps out. The therapist looks out the window and says, "Plop."

Therapists are also taught to be nonjudgmental and refrain from imposing their values and biases onto their patients. Anna Freud (1946) advised the competent therapist to remain equidistant from the patient's id, ego, and superego. By this she meant that the therapist does not prohibit or criticize (is not a superego), does not sanction sexual or aggressive gratifications (is not an id), and does not reinforce defensive operations (is not an ego). This is sometimes difficult to carry out in practice.

Mr. James came to see a therapist and shyly reported that he loved dogs, as a matter of fact he had sex with them. The therapist commented, "Dogs are man's best friend." Mr. James went on, "But doctor, I also have sex with cats." "Don't berate yourself," said the therapist; "cats, pussies, very libidinal." The patient went on to report having sex with horses and cows, and again the therapist was non-judgmental and accepting, commenting on the beautiful lines of the horse, and the cows giving milk. Finally the patient admitted, "Doctor, I also have sex with chickens." "Chickens?" the doctor exclaimed. "Feh, feh, feh, get out of here!"

When a practitioner is known to enact the role of omniscient adviser, he gets many interesting results.

A young man was born with a golden screw in his belly button. He was always embarrassed about it, wouldn't take gym with his class or get undressed where he might be seen. He went on to college and did well. He fell in love with a girl he wished he could marry but couldn't imagine how he could do that with his golden screw. He confessed his problem to a friend who suggested that a psychiatrist might help. When the young man told the doctor his problem, the therapist said, "Tonight you will have a dream. In it you will see a fluffy pink cloud. Reach into it and you will find an ivory-handled screwdriver. Unscrew the golden screw." That night the young man has the dream about the pink cloud and the ivory-handled screw-driver, which he uses to unscrew the golden screw from his belly button. When he wakes up in the morning, he remembers his dream, looks down at his belly button and sees that the golden screw is gone! He is so happy he jumps out of bed and his ass falls off.

The well-known entertainer of the 1930s and 1940s, Eddie Cantor, liked to tell stories of psychiatrists conversing with each other.

One psychiatrist said to another, "You think you got problems? I've been doing some tests with my patients. I ask them three questions." "What kind of questions?" the other psychiatrist wanted to know. "The first one is, 'What would you say if I asked you what wears a skirt and employs the lips to give pleasure?'" "I'd say a Scottish bagpiper," answered his fellow professional. "Right. The second question is, 'What has streamlined curves and arouses the most basic instincts in man?'" "A roller coaster." "Right, now here's the third question. 'What's warm and soft and a pleasure to share a bed with?'" "A hot-water bottle." "What else? But you should hear the strange answers my patients give!"

Responding to the Process

When people have been in psychotherapy for a while, they respond to the process in many ways. On the positive side, they find themselves becoming more loving and less hateful; more sexual and less inhibited; more communicative and less withholding; more object-related and less narcissistic; more creative and less mechanical; more productive and less bored and boring. Yet, the psychotherapeutic process introduces new ways of conceptualizing life that are not always easy to master.

> A patient told his therapist after several months of treatment, "In the past when people asked, 'How are you?' I'd say 'Fine.' Now I say to myself, 'I wonder what they meant by that?'"

Another patient said, "I used to think a couch was used for making love instead of just telling about it." And still another patient mused, "Psychotherapy has been a wonderful invention; it makes simple people feel they are complicated." And then there was the patient who reflected that he struggled enormously to give up alcohol. Now whenever he gets suicidal and swallows a bottle of sleeping pills, he calls his psychiatrist who recommends, "Have a few drinks and get some rest."

Self-help

During the last two decades when many different forms of psychotherapy have been questioned, self-help organizations have proliferated. Alcoholics Anonymous has been more popular than ever. Even a casual observer of the therapeutic scene has noted the flourishing of such organizations as Gamblers Anonymous, Overeaters Anonymous, Wife Abusers Anonymous, and so on. I suspect that someday soon somebody is going to start an organization called Psychotherapy Anonymous for all those souls who tried it but came out dissatisfied. Although psychotherapy has demonstrated that it can help many individuals, it is far from a cure-all. Self-help groups have become so popular that they have their own literature. As with any phenomenon that involves people and their problems, jokes have evolved on self-help procedures. I wonder if a friend was kidding me when he told me, "I went to a bookstore and asked for the self-help section. The woman behind the counter said, 'If I told you, that would defeat the whole purpose.'" A patient supposedly told her therapist, "I was going to buy a copy of *The Power of Positive Thinking* and then I thought, 'What the hell good would that do?'" A patient told me he read a self-help book and the author concluded that all of the problems of the world can be subsumed under the categories of "ignorance" and "apathy." I asked what he thought about that and he replied, "I don't know and I don't care."

The comedian Steve Martin commented, "I have a new book coming out. It's one of those self-help deals; it's called *How to Get Along with Everyone*. I wrote it with this other asshole."

> There was an extremely modest psychotherapist by the name of Strange. He was so modest that in his will he asked that his name should not be inscribed on his tombstone. So, when he died a few years later, his best friend respected his wishes, and his tombstone read:

"Here Lies a Competent Psychotherapist." But then people would pass by his grave and say, "That's Strange!"

I was told that when Mel Brooks, the actor and comedian, ended his personal analysis he had an interesting comment to make. I can't think of a better way to end this chapter than to quote him, "As long as the world is turning and spinning we're gonna be dizzy and we're gonna make mistakes."

Epilogue:

He Who Laughs

Last . . .

As I take leave of you, my reader, I would like to share some of my free associations. My first is from an old Indian saying, "Sorrow shared is halved and joy shared is doubled." This saying mirrors my state of mind as I say goodbye to you. I am sad our journey is ending but by telling that, the letdown for me tends to lessen. The joy I have derived from sharing over three hundred jokes with you has been enormous.

I believe the Indian saying I recalled is one that has much value for psychotherapists. We all are aware of the fact that when our patients share their sadness with us and tell us about distressful thoughts and feelings, they do feel less tormented. However, the therapeutic literature has had very little to say about sharing our patients' joys with them. Most of us are so preoccupied with pathology, maladaptation, conflict, anxiety, and the rest that we have not thought enough about how to respond to our patients' positive experiences. All too often we mistakenly equate a happy patient with a resistive one.

Some patients, some of the time, can accentuate the positive in order to eliminate looking at the negative. Just as we do give tacit approval by verbalizing "Mmm" when a patient works through something and has a valuable insight, it would also seem therapeutic to "Mmm" a patient's occasional laugh as well. It may not always be a sign of unprofessionalism to laugh with the patient when he or she is experiencing true joy and thereby demonstrate that a serious, disciplined relationship has room for laughs, too.

As I reflect on the notion of laughter in psychotherapy, my next association is to a statement made by the former Prime Minister of England, Margaret Thatcher. She said, "Standing in the middle of the road is very dangerous; you get knocked down by the traffic from both sides." I think of Thatcher's statement now because it reflects the position many therapists, including myself, have had about the meaning and purpose of jokes in human intercourse. As I suggested in this book's preface, since Sigmund Freud did his careful study on the subject of jokes, we clinicians have not added very much to his conceptualizations. Although we are mature enough to consider and reconsider what we can add to and subtract from Freud when it comes to issues like object relations, the super-ego, transference and countertransference, resistance and counterresistance, religion, love, sex, parents and children, art, the occult, and civilization and its discontents, why can't we do the same with wit, humor, laughter, and jokes?

When I was doing research for this book, I came across a statement by the progressive educator Herb Gardner, who said, "Once you get people laughing, they're listening and you can tell them almost anything." The reason this statement attracted me is that, like the jokes I appreciate, it stirred up something familiar. In teaching and supervising, I have often found that when students and supervisees are laughing, they can listen with less resistance. I have tried in this book to utilize the joke as a means of conveying some of my notions on marriage, sex, parent–child relations, religious and racial matters, and on psychotherapy. I am hopeful that this format will be of some assistance to other educators in the mental health professions so they can fuse wit and humor with serious reflection on therapeutic matters. Perhaps all of us can better communicate with each other if we try to sense the humor in human interactions.

I hope that our journey together, dear reader, has helped you have more appreciation for the joke as another road to the unconscious. I predict that the joke will someday have almost as much value for us as the dream. Then we will say to our patients, "Tell me whatever comes to your mind—your feelings, thoughts, memories, fantasies, dreams, and jokes." Maybe this addition will help us learn more about our patients' dynamic unconscious, clarify certain transference and countertransference issues, and strengthen the therapeutic alliance. Perhaps, too, more of us may discriminately use humor as an occasional accompaniment to our interpretations. If, at times, jokes are used as a resistance and/or counterresistance in the treatment, as Anna Freud suggested, let us better understand how and why our patients, or we, resist—rather than just try to overcome the resistance quickly.

As I finalize this epilogue, I think of the many wonderful relatives, friends, and colleagues who have traded jokes with me over many decades. When I recall some of those who have died, I am reminded of their jokes and some of my sadness turns to a bit of gladness. I then think of Sigmund Freud's statement to Theodor Reik when they parted for the last time, "People who belong together do not have to be glued together."

On many occasions, jokes have helped me feel closer to individuals. Jokes seem to provide a means of capturing mutually positive emotions between people. My mother-in-law, who loved and was loved by many people, until her dying day at the age of 90 always had a joke to tell. Often she would call on the telephone, tell a joke, and then hang up. When you called her back and said, "Hey, you told me a funny joke and then hung up. Why?" she would reply, "I like to leave them laughing."

References

Ables, B. (1977). *Therapy for Couples*. San Francisco: Jossey-Bass.

Allen, W. (1971). *Getting Even*. New York: Warner.

——— (1975). *Without Feathers*. New York: Warner.

——— (1980) *Side Effects*. New York: Random House.

Barker, R. (1987). *The Social Work Dictionary*. Silver Spring, MD: National Association of Social Workers.

Bartusis, M. (1978). *Every Other Man*. New York: Dutton.

Bergler, E. (1956). *Laughter and the Sense of Humor*. New York: Grune & Stratton.

Beron, L. (1944). Fathers as clients of a child guidance clinic. *Smith College Studies in Social Work* 14:351–366.

Block, J. (1978). *The Other Man, The Other Woman*. New York: Grosset & Dunlap.

Burgum, M. (1942). The father gets worse: a child guidance problem. *American Journal of Orthopsychiatry*, 32:569–584.

Chasseguet-Smirgel, J. (1988). The triumph of humor. In *Fantasy, Myth, and Reality: Essays in Honor of Jacob Arlow*, ed. A. Blum, V. Kramer, A. K. Richards, and A. D. Richards, pp. 197–213. Madison, CT: International Universities Press.

Clark, R. (1980). *Freud: The Man and the Cause*. New York: Random House.

DeBurger, J. (1978). *Marriage Today*. Cambridge, MA: Schenkman.

DeMause, L. (1982). *Foundations of Psychohistory*. New York: Creative Roots.

Despert, L. (1965). *The Emotionally Disturbed Child: Then and Now*. New York: Robert Brunner.

Dicks, H. (1967). *Marital Tensions*. New York: Basic Books.

Eisenstein, V. (1956). *Neurotic Interaction in Marriage*. New York: Basic Books.

Erikson, E. (1950). *Childhood and Society*. New York: W. W. Norton.

Evans, R. (1964). *Conversations with Carl Jung*. Princeton, NJ: Van Nostrand Reinhold.

Fenichel, O. (1945). *The Psychoanalytic Theory of Neurosis*. New York: W. W. Norton.

Fine, R. (1979). *The History of Psychoanalysis*. New York: Columbia University Press.

_____ (1985). *The Meaning of Love in Human Experience*. New York: Wiley.

Fraser, A. (1993). *The Wives of Henry VIII*. New York: Alfred A. Knopf.

Freud, A. (1946). *The Ego and the Mechanisms of Defense*. New York: International Universities Press.

_____ (1965). *Normality and Pathology in Childhood*. New York: International Universities Press.

Freud, S. (1905). Jokes and their relation to the unconscious. *Standard Edition* 8:3–236.

_____ (1909). Notes upon a case of obsessional neurosis. *Standard Edition* 10:153–249.

_____ (1914). On narcissism. *Standard Edition* 14:67–102.

_____ (1919). From the history of an infantile neurosis. *Standard Edition* 17:7–71.

_____ (1937a) Analysis terminable and interminable. *Standard Edition* 23:209–253.

_____ (1937b) Moses and monotheism. *Standard Edition* 23:7–137.

_____ (1939). An outline of psychoanalysis. *Standard Edition* 23:144–171.

Fromm, E. (1950). *Man's Religions*. New York: Macmillan.

Gay, P. (1979). *Freud, Jews, and Other Germans: Masters and Victims in Modernist Culture*. Oxford, England: Oxford University Press.

Gorer, G. (1948). *The American People*. New York: W. W. Norton.

Greenson, R. (1967). *The Technique and Practice of Psychoanalysis*. New York: International Universities Press.

Grotjahn, M. (1957). *Beyond Laughter*. New York: McGraw-Hill.

Grunebaum, H. (1962). Group psychotherapy of fathers: problems of technique. *British Journal of Medical Psychology* 35:147–154.

Grunebaum, H., and Christ, J. (1976). *Contemporary Marriage: Structure, Dynamics, Therapy.* Boston: Little, Brown.

Grunebaum, H., and Strean, H. (1970). Some considerations on the therapeutic neglect of fathers in child guidance. In *New Approaches in Child Guidance,* ed. H. Strean, pp. 178–193. Metuchen, NJ: Scarecrow.

Hartmann, H. (1958). *Ego Psychology and the Problem of Adaptation.* New York: International Universities Press.

Holland, N. (1982). *Laughing: A Psychology of Humor.* Ithaca, NY: Cornell University Press.

Hunt, M. (1969). *The Affair.* Bergenfield, NJ: New American Library.

Jersild, A. (1949). *Child Psychology.* New York: Prentice-Hall.

Jones, E. (1953). *The Life and Work of Sigmund Freud.* 3 vols. (1953–1957). New York: Basic Books.

Kaplan, H. (1974). *The New Sex Therapy.* New York: Brunner/Mazel.

Karasu, T., and Socarides, C. (1979). *On Sexuality: Psychoanalytic Observations.* New York: International Universities Press.

Kaye, E. (1980). *Cross Currents: Children, Families and Religion.* New York: Clarkson N. Potter.

Klein, M. (1957). *Envy and Gratitude.* New York: Basic Books.

Koch, L., and Koch, J. (1976). *The Marriage Savers.* New York: Coward, McCann, & Geoghegan.

Kris, E. (1938). Ego development and the comic. In *Psychoanalytic Explorations in Art,* ed. E. Kris, pp. 204–216. New York: International Universities Press, 1952.

_____ (1952). *Psychoanalytic Explorations in Art.* New York: International Universities Press.

Langley, R., and Levy, R. (1977). *Wife Beating: The Silent Crisis.* New York: Dutton.

Legman, G. (1968). *The Rationale of the Dirty Joke: An Analysis of Sexual Humor.* New York: Grove.

Levenson, S. (1979). *You Don't Have to Be in Who's Who to Know What's What.* New York: Simon & Schuster.

Mason, J. (1987). *The World According to Me.* New York: Simon & Schuster.

Masters, W., and Johnson, V. (1970). *Human Sexual Inadequacy.* Boston: Little, Brown.

Mead, M. (1967). Sexual freedom and cultural change. Paper presented at the forum, The Pill and the Puritan Ethic. San Francisco State College, San Francisco, CA, February 10.

Miller, A. (1964). *After the Fall.* New York: Viking.

Moore, B., and Fine, B. (1990). *Psychoanalytic Terms and Concepts.* New Haven, CT: Yale University Press.

Myrdal, G. (1944). *An American Dilemma*. New York: Harper.

Nass, J. (1949). *Man's Religions*. New York: Macmillan.

O'Neill, N., and O'Neill, G. (1972). *Open Marriage*. New York: M. Evans.

Oring, E. (1984). *The Jokes of Sigmund Freud*. Philadelphia: University of Pennsylvania Press.

Oxford Dictionary of Quotations (1992). 4th ed. Oxford, England: Oxford University Press.

Pine, F. (1985). *Developmental Theory and Clinical Process*. New Haven, CT: Yale University Press.

Poland, W. (1990). The gift of laughter: on the development of a sense of humor in clinical psychoanalysis. *Psychoanalytic Quarterly* 59:197–225.

Reich, W. (1949). *Character Analysis*. 3rd ed. New York: Orgone Institute Press.

Reik, T. (1948). *Masochism in Modern Man*. New York: Farrar & Straus.

—— (1954). Freud and Jewish wit. *Psychoanalysis* 2:12–20.

—— (1962). *Jewish Wit*. New York: Gamut.

Rosten, L. (1961). *The Return of Hyman Kaplan*. New York: Harper.

—— (1968). *The Joys of Yiddish*. New York: McGraw-Hill.

—— (1985). *Giant Book of Laughter*. New York: Bonanza.

Roustang, F. (1987). How do you make a paranoiac laugh? *Modern Language Notes* 102:707–718.

Russell, B. (1929). *Marriage and Morals*. New York: Liveright.

Sachs, H. (1946). *Freud: Master and Friend*. Cambridge, MA: Harvard University Press.

Satow, R. (1991). Three perspectives on humor and laughing: classical, object relations, and self psychology. *Group* 15:242–245.

Sims, C. (1992). Toy makers meet the inner child. *The New York Times*, December 27, p. 12.

Sklare, M. (1960). *The Jews: Social Patterns of an American Group*. Glencoe, IL: The Free Press.

Smith, R. (1992). *The Comedy Quote Dictionary*. New York: Doubleday.

Spalding, H. (1978). *American Jewish Humor*. Middle Village, NY: Jonathan David.

Spitz, R. (1959). *A Genetic Field Theory of Ego Formation*. New York: International Universities Press.

Sternbach, O. (1947). Arrested ego development and its treatment in conduct disorders and neuroses of childhood. *The Nervous Child* 6:306–317.

Stone, L. (1992). *Road to Divorce*. New York: Oxford University Press.

Strean, H. (1962). A means of involving fathers in family treatment:

guidance groups for fathers. *American Journal of Orthopsychiatry* 32:714–727.

———— (1979). *Psychoanalytic Theory and Social Work Practice.* New York: The Free Press.

———— (1980). *The Extramarital Affair.* New York: The Free Press.

———— (1983). *The Sexual Dimension.* New York: The Free Press.

———— (1985). *Resolving Marital Conflicts.* New York: Wiley.

———— (1991). *Behind the Couch.* New York: Continuum.

———— (1993). *Resolving Counterresistances in Psychotherapy.* New York: Brunner/Mazel.

Strean, H., and Freeman, L. (1991). *Our Wish to Kill.* New York: St. Martin's Press.

Sullivan, H. (1953). *The Interpersonal Theory of Psychiatry.* New York: W. W. Norton.

Sussman, M. (1992). *A Curious Calling.* Northvale, NJ: Jason Aronson.

Telushkin, J. (1992). *Jewish Humor.* New York: William Morrow.

Thickett, M. (1983). *Outrageously Offensive Jokes.* New York: Pocket Books.

Waelder, R. (1933). The psychoanalytic theory of play. *Psychoanalytic Quarterly* 2:208–224.

The Winston Dictionary (1943). Philadelphia: The John Winston Company.

Wolfenstein, M. (1954). *Children's Humor: A Psychological Analysis.* Glencoe, IL: The Free Press.

Zwerling, I. (1955). The favorite joke in diagnostic and therapeutic interviewing. *Psychoanalytic Quarterly* 24:104–114.

Index